THE
Francophone
World

Francophone Cultures and Literatures

Michael G. Paulson & Tamara Alvarez-Detrell
General Editors

Vol. 20

PETER LANG
New York • Washington, D.C./Baltimore • Bern
Frankfurt am Main • Berlin • Brussels • Vienna • Oxford

THE
Francophone
World

CULTURAL ISSUES AND PERSPECTIVES

Edited by
Michelle Beauclair

PETER LANG
New York • Washington, D.C./Baltimore • Bern
Frankfurt am Main • Berlin • Brussels • Vienna • Oxford

Library of Congress Cataloging-in-Publication Data

The Francophone world: cultural issues and perspectives /
[edited by] Michelle Beauclair.
p. cm. — (Francophone cultures and literatures; v. 20)
Includes bibliographical references.
1. French literature—French-speaking countries—History and criticism.
2. French-speaking countries—Civilization. 3. Language and culture—
French-speaking countries. 4. Ethnicity—French-speaking
countries. I. Beauclair, Michelle. II. Series.
PQ3897 .F733   840.9—dc21   2002021414
ISBN 978-0-8204-3739-2
ISSN 1077-0186

Die Deutsche Bibliothek-CIP-Einheitsaufnahme

Beauclair, Michelle:
The Francophone world: cultural issues and perspectives /
ed. by: Michelle Beauclair.
–New York; Washington, D.C./Baltimore; Bern;
Frankfurt am Main; Berlin; Brussels; Vienna; Oxford: Lang.
(Francophone cultures and literatures; Vol. 20)
ISBN 978-0-8204-3739-2

Cover art by Julien Maingois

The paper in this book meets the guidelines for permanence and durability
of the Committee on Production Guidelines for Book Longevity
of the Council of Library Resources.

Printed in the United States of America

 # DEDICATION

In memory of Elaine Marks, Germaine Brée Professor of French and Women's Studies at the University of Wisconsin-Madison, who influenced many of the contributors to this book.

 # ACKNOWLEDGMENTS

I wish to thank the contributors to this book for their fine research, their excellent essays, and their valuable insights. I would also like to thank Heidi Burns at Peter Lang Publishing for her oversight of this project. I wish to express my appreciation also to the general editors, Michael G. Paulson and Tamara Alvarez-Detrell, for encouraging the inclusion of this volume in the Francophone Cultures and Literatures series. I am grateful to Dan Dootson and Stephen Latshaw in Media Services at Edmonds Community College for their assistance in document conversion and especially to Julien Maingois for the time and creative energy he contributed to the cover design. Finally, I wish to extend a very special thanks to Kamie Kahlo of Green Tea Design for the formatting of this text.

CONTENTS

Introduction, *Michelle Beauclair* 1

Part I   Francophone Issues in West Africa 9
    1 Media and Cultures in Francophone West Africa:
       Journalists, Chiefs, Elders, and Marginals
       Alain Péricard 11
    2 Tradition, Modernity, and the Clash of Cultures in African
       Society: The Example of Burkina Faso
       Paschal B. Kyiiripuo Kyoore 31
    3 The Special Status of Senegal and the Emergence of
       Women Writers
       Susan Stringer 49

Part II   Francophone Issues in North Africa and France 67
    4 North Africans in France: A Crisis in Cultural Identity—
       Tahar Ben Jelloun's *Les Raisins de la galère*
       Sylvie Charron and Sue Huseman 69

Part III Francophone Issues in the Caribbean 89
    5 Martinique: Culture and Identity
       Debra L. Anderson 91
    6 Staging Decolonization: The Theater of Aimé Césaire
       Timothy Scheie 105
    7 South America's "Guyane": Model of Francophone Diversity
       Marcia G. Parker and Beverley G. David 121

Part IV Francophone Issues in North America 143
    8 "Je me souviens": Quebec's Literary and Linguistic Journey
       Marie-Paule Méda 145

x

Contents

9 The Francophone Presence in the Northeastern United States
   Janet L. Shideler 161

Contributors 173

 INTRODUCTION

Michelle Beauclair

The Francophone World: Cultural Issues and Perspectives grew out of the necessity for relevant, current materials written in English to broaden cultural understanding and to enhance discussions among students taking either general cultural diversity courses, world literature courses, or advanced French or francophone literature and culture courses. Since the majority of articles and books on the subject of francophone cultures and literature are written, understandably, in French, this textbook seeks to reach students who are interested in diverse cultures, but who might not have the fluency to grasp in-depth concepts and presentations in French.

In a broader sense, *The Francophone World* offers information on the cultural production and the challenges faced within non-European countries where French is spoken as well as among different ethnic groups within France itself. With new technologies and the increasingly global economy, it is crucial that today's students, the future actors in this global community, have an appreciation and an awareness of diverse cultures. To that end, recent trends in American education have been focusing more and more upon non-Western cultures and diverse cultures within the North American continent itself. Most French departments and programs throughout the country have embraced and encouraged this trend by expanding their programs to include some study of the cultural, literary, and film production in French outside of France and outside of Europe.

In an effort to introduce students to the francophone world, this book focuses mainly upon those non-European areas outside of France where the use of French is the most concentrated and even contentious. The essays are divided into four separate sections on francophone cultures: the first section explores the French influence in West Africa, the second section examines the plight of North African immigrants living in France, the third focuses upon the diversity of cultures within the Caribbean, and the forth section treats francophone communities in North America including Quebec. The approach is interdisciplinary, thus providing a more complete, well-rounded view of the cultures in question.

Furthermore, this interdisciplinary approach lends itself to a broader humanities format and appeals to students with a variety of interests.

To begin, it is necessary to define what is meant by the phrase, "the francophone world." The French have a term, *la francophonie*, which can alternately mean the geographical regions of the world where French is spoken, the entire populace of French speakers worldwide, or even those countries with close cultural and historic ties to France who participate in francophone summits. Whether French is a primary, a secondary, or even an administrative language in these areas, they all share some cultural or linguistic kinship to France. Thus, the term *la francophonie* could also refer to a sort of conceptual or "spiritual" community, as the Senegalese writer and statesman Léopold Sédar Senghor once described it.[1]

Beyond this unifying thread, however, there lies a remarkable diversity within francophone communities. This book will introduce readers to some of the different French-speaking communities around the world and offer a perspective on the cultures that have developed either around the legacy of French exploratory and trade efforts in the early sixteenth, seventeenth, and eighteenth centuries in North America and the Caribbean or as the result of French colonizing efforts in the nineteenth and twentieth centuries in Africa and Asia.

Any attempt to define the francophone world in geographical or even geopolitical terms would show that francophone nations or regions of the world outside of France, that is, those for whom French is either a primary or a secondary language, are present on virtually every continent. In Europe, many of France's neighbors are fully or partially francophone including Belgium, Switzerland, Luxembourg, the principalities of Monaco and Andorra, and the Channel Islands of Guernsey and Jersey.[2]

In North America, Canada is officially bilingual, with French being the sole official language of the province of Quebec. New Brunswick is Canada's only officially bilingual province with approximately 34% of its population being native French speakers. While the vast majority of Canada's roughly 7 million native speakers of French come from Quebec (around 6 million), the rest are scattered throughout the other nine provinces and three territories. Close to half a million of the French speakers outside of Quebec reside in Ontario. French is also widely spoken by descendants of the Acadian population in the maritime Canadian province of Nova Scotia.[3]

In addition, the islands of St. Pierre and Miguelon, off the eastern coast of Canada, are francophone. These two islands are overseas territories of France that maintain a status much like that of Guam to the United States. France's overseas territories or *territoires d'outre mer (T.O.M.)* have fewer rights than one would find in a French province, but most receive some economic assistance from France.[4]

The northeastern United States could be considered francophone in a historic sense in that many French Canadians left Quebec and migrated to Vermont, Maine, New Hampshire, and Massachusetts, bringing their language and culture with them. To the south, the state of Louisiana and its principal city, New Orleans, are thought of in many respects as culturally francophone. Claimed for France by Cavalier de la Salle during the reign of Louis the XIV, Louisiana eventually became the home of many of the Acadians who were forced out of Canada by the English in 1755. New Orleans, founded in 1718, has also managed to retain its French flavor to the present day in areas of the city such as the famous French Quarter.

In the Caribbean, French is the official language of Haiti and of the islands of Guadeloupe and Martinique, two of France's overseas departments or *départements d'outre mer (D.O.M.)*. Overseas departments are roughly the equivalent of states or provinces that are not located on the mainland, much like Hawaii and Alaska in the United States. These departments have the same rights as French provinces, including representation in the French parliament, and they maintain the same educational system. The use of French in the Caribbean extends to the islands of Dominica and St. Lucia and can be heard as well on the islands of St. Martin and St. Barthélemy among others.

Across the Caribbean, on the South American continent, French is the official language of French Guiana. French Guiana—like Guadeloupe and Martinique, its Caribbean neighbors to the northwest—is yet another department of France.

Much more visible than the francophone presence in the Americas is the francophone presence in Africa. French is one of the predominant languages, along with Arabic, in the North African nations of Tunisia, Morocco, and Algeria, although the status of the French language in this latter country is precarious at present due to the current civil unrest in that nation and the polarizing effect of the French language within it. In West Africa, French is one of the official languages of Benin, Burkina Faso, Côte d'Ivoire (formerly the Ivory Coast), Equitorial Guinea, Guinea, Mali, Niger, Senegal, and Togo. It is also one of the principal languages of Mauritania. In Central Africa, French is spoken in Cameroon, the Central African Republic, Chad, Congo, and Gabon. In addition, the Democratic Republic of the Congo (formerly Zaire), Rwanda, and Burundi are francophone as a result of Belgian rather than French colonization. French is also one of the official languages of Djibouti in East Africa.

French remains a principle language of the Indian Ocean islands of Madagascar and Reunion (a department of France), as well as in the Comoros islands, Mayotte (a French overseas territory), Mauritius, and the Seychelles. In the southern Indian Ocean, the French claim a portion of Antarctica, the "Adelie Land," for scientific research, along with the islands of Amsterdam, St. Paul,

Kerguelen, and Crozet, which are part of France's overseas territories.

The use of French extends even further. It is a primary language of the Pacific Ocean islands of French Polynesia, New Caledonia, and Wallis and Futuna, all of which are French overseas territories. On the Pacific Ocean island of Vanuatu, fully one-third of the inhabitants are native French speakers.

In addition to the lengthy list of nations and states whose predominant languages include French, the francophone world includes many nations that have close historic, cultural, or educational ties to France. In Asia, for example, in the area that was formerly known as French Indochina, the French left their mark not only on some of the architecture and urban planning, but also on the institutions of higher learning in the countries of Laos, Cambodia, and Vietnam.[5] Similarly, several countries in Eastern Europe share cultural ties with France due to the presence of elite French schools in those countries. In the Middle East, Egypt and to a lesser extent Syria both have a sizable number of fluent French-speakers among their educated population. After World War I, a League of Nations mandate put Lebanon under French administration. Lebanon remained a French mandate until 1943. As a result, the French language and the French-language press continue to have a strong presence there.

Many of these culturally connected francophone nations are participating members in francophone summits that are administered by the *Agence Inter-gouvernementale de la Francophonie* and the *Organisation Internationale de la Francophonie*. The participating member nations at these francophone summits share a desire to be linked with France and the broader francophone community both for the promotion and preservation of the French language and culture, as well as for reasons of economic and political solidarity. Another stated goal of these francophone conferences is the promotion of peace, cooperation, and understanding among educators, business people, politicians, and the media in the member nations.[6] While not having significant French-speaking populations, Albania, Bulgaria, the Czech Republic, Israel, Lithuania, Macedonia, Moldavia, Romania, Poland, and Slovenia are all participants—whether as member nations or as observer states—at the francophone conferences. Similarly, many African nations with francophone neighbor countries also participate in these summits including Cape Verde, Guinea-Bissau, and Sao Tome and Principe.

One of the driving forces behind this solidarity movement among member nations of the francophone world is to preserve the French language and culture in the face of an increasingly global economic community where English is the primary language and vehicle of culture. At present, it is estimated that French is ranked well behind English, Spanish, Mandarin Chinese, and Indonesian in terms of the number of primary speakers.[7]

Yet, while ranking behind some of the other major world languages, French still has an import beyond the strict tabulation of the number of speakers. Like

English and Spanish, the use of French is not restricted to one or two countries. In addition, the French language has historical significance. It was the language of diplomacy in the eighteenth and nineteenth centuries, much like English is today. It was also the language of the elite educated classes in a number of European countries and the language of the Russian courts at the time of Catherine the Great. There is a certain prestige that is associated with the French language and culture deriving in part from France's renown in art, literature, cuisine, wine, fashion, and perfume. Even today, French remains one of the most studied languages in the United States and Europe.[8]

Perhaps some of its significance, and some of what is at stake in the whole movement toward francophone unity, could be explained in part by the idea of a conceptual or cultural bond that many speakers of French around the world feel they share. This is due in large measure to the fact that everywhere the French went in an effort to colonize and "civilize," they also set up schools that were modeled after the French educational system and priorities. It has been said that one of the most distinguishing features of French colonization was its distinct military character. Still, the more enduring elements of that colonial era were the educational institutions that were put into place in the colonies. The French wanted to be known as the educators to the world, and they made that a primary focus. As the historian Raymond Betts so aptly points out in *Tricouleur*, his historical account of French colonization, for the country which produced the Declaration of the Rights of Man, the politicians back in Paris in the 1800s needed just such a "mission" to justify their presence in foreign lands.[9]

While the current struggle to preserve the French language and culture in the face of the English language and associated cultural values is a relatively modern quest, the whole idea of cultural standards transmitted by the very use of language is, of course, not a new one. French missionaries themselves, in setting up schools in French Indochina, transcribed one of the Vietnamese languages into Roman characters fearing the Asian characters as carriers of Eastern thought.[10]

The fact that language, culture, history, and certain cultural values are linked has taken a sadly ironic and poignant turn in the case of one "francophone" nation, Algeria. While Algeria forcibly expelled the French in 1962 after roughly 130 years of colonization, today some Algerian intellectuals brandish the use of French and the ideals of a secular, democratic society. They do this to oppose an increasingly zealous and radical Islamic fundamentalist regime that has set the educational institutions in that nation back decades. Over the course of the past thirty years, the government has tried to eliminate the use of French in schools in favor of instruction in Arabic.[11]

Elsewhere, the linguistic and cultural nemesis of the francophone movement is, in many ways, the English language and what has come to be called,

"American cultural imperialism." Evidence of this anglophobia on the part of many speakers of French can be found in institutions such as the *Académie Française*, whose mission it is to keep the French language pure, as much as possible, from the influence of other languages, in particular, English. Although the *Académie Française* has been in existence since 1635, nonetheless, today it has the nearly insurmountable task of contending with new technological terms that are rapidly being created.[12] Across the Atlantic, in Quebec, there is the infamous *Office de la Langue Française* whose responsibility it is to ensure that, by law, French maintains a superior status in industry, government, education, and most visibly, in advertising within the province. On all commercial signs in Quebec, for example, the French lettering must be at least twice the size of the English script.[13] In the international realm, well over a thousand *Alliance Française* chapters exist for the express purpose of promoting and teaching the French language and culture.

These are but three of the institutions worldwide that are perhaps less important in what they accomplish in a concrete, tangible sense than in what they stand for conceptually. The very fact that they exist points to a deeper, more fundamental concern. With the increasing dominance of English as the world language, with its predominance in the field of information technology, and with the mass exportation of American culture, speakers of French — once the language of diplomacy and international law — sense that their culture and language are vulnerable.

France, of course, is not alone in its bid to preserve and promote its unique culture. It is well known that Canada and even Australia have enacted measures to promote their own artists, films, and magazines so as to withstand the popularity of movies and music from the United States. Still, in a country such as France with its particular attachment to its history and language, this outside cultural influence is seemingly felt more acutely than it is elsewhere.

Nevertheless, it would be inaccurate to say that the whole concept of francophone unity or some bond between speakers of French is a modern phenomenon conceived in reaction to the omnipresence of American popular culture. The francophone solidarity movement can be traced back to the time of decolonization when, in the 1960s, francophone associations were formed among educators and universities. Even so, it is interesting to note that, if viewed in this way, France's current bid toward francophone unity is not unlike efforts by those ethnic groups in the former French colonies to maintain aspects of their own indigenous cultures in the very midst of French attempts to acculturate them.

Ironically, another perceived challenge to the French language is coming from within France itself. The use of regional languages, long discouraged in France, is reemerging. In Brittany, in northwest France, an estimated 200,000 to 500,000 people speak the traditional Breton language, a language of Celtic origin. A recent debate about whether the French government should finance Breton immersion schools has some worried that other regional and cultural groups, such as North African immigrants, might also seek to teach their languages in the schools.[14]

Clearly, beyond the challenge of preserving a "distinct" linguistic and cultural identity in a changing world, francophone regions face additional and even more significant challenges, both individually and collectively. It is hoped that by learning about the francophone world, readers of this book will gain greater insight into diverse cultural issues worldwide and a clearer perspective on the blend of cultures within their own communities and nations.

An inscription on the wall of the Intercultural Center at Georgetown University by the French anthropologist and philosopher Pierre Teilhard de Chardin reads, "The age of nations is past. Its remains for us now, if we do not wish to perish, to set aside the ancient prejudices and build the earth." In light of the tragic events of September 11, 2001, it is hoped that this text can contribute, in some small way, to the advancement of world peace.

NOTES

1   Léopold Sédar Senghor, address, University of Laval, 1966.

2   *The CIA World Factbook*, 2001, 2 December 2001 <http://www.odci.gov/cia/publications factbook>.

3   Mireille Duteil, "Francophonie: La Revanche des Acadiens," *Le Point* 27 Aug. 1999: 42–45.

4   See Jean Thumerelle, "La Population des DOM-TOM: originalité et diversité des sociétés de la France d'outre-mer," in *La France dans le monde*, ed. Gabriel Wackermann (Paris: Nathan, 1992), 93–96.

5   For additional information, see Nicola Cooper, *France in Indochina: Colonial Encounters* (Oxford: Berg, 2001).

6   See, for example, Paul Guilbert, "Chirac exalte la coopération," *Le Figaro*, 8 Sept. 1999.

7   See Alain Huetz de Lemps, "Introduction au monde francophone," *La France dans le monde*, ed. Gabriel Wackermann (Paris: Nathan, 1992), 7–8.

8   For more information, see "Dumbstruck," *The Economist*, 14 Jan. 1995, and Tan Vinh, "French Schools? Mais Oui!," *The Seattle Times*, 20 Sept. 1999: B1–B2.

9   See Raymond Betts, *Tricouleur: The French Overseas Empire* (London: Gordon and Cremonesi, 1978).

10   Ibid.

11   See Khalida Messaoudi and Elisabeth Schemla, *Unbowed: An Algerian Woman Confronts Islamic Fundamentalism*, trans. Anne C. Vila (Philadelphia: University of Pennsylvania Press, 1998).

12   For additional information on the *Académie Française*, see John-Thor Dahlburg, "40 'Immortals' Immersed in Politics," *The Seattle Times*, 18 January 1998.

13   "War of Words," *Sixty Minutes*, narr. Morley Safer, CBS, 8 Feb. 1998.

14   "The Breton Language," *Weekend Edition Sunday*, National Public Radio, 2 Dec. 2001.

PART ONE

Francophone Issues in West Africa

❖❖ CHAPTER ONE
❖ Media and Cultures in Francophone West Africa: Journalists, Chiefs, Elders, and Marginals

Alain Péricard

Francophone West Africa, as its name suggests, is defined today by the use of a language imposed after the French colonial invasion. Other than language, the nine countries that comprise francophone West Africa use similar administrative models and institutions,[1] as well as intellectual and commercial exchange channels that all remain largely oriented to the former "métropole." These countries' mass media, state-run for the most part, have also been modeled after the centralized French example. Their respective infrastructures have been set up by France, on whom they depend for hardware, as well as for a significant portion of programming (Tudesq, 1992; Bourgault, 1995).

Yet the francophone media of West Africa also reveal some of the cultural singularities of the heterogeneous societies that have co-existed in the same vast territory for many centuries. How culture and communication interact in this setting is the focus of this essay. It will be addressed on three different levels: first, the imposition of French perspectives of Africa through texts and the establishment of a media system; second, the transformation of these perspectives by the elites controlling the francophone West African states; and, finally, the maintenance and the transformation of indigenous communication networks as a means of resistance to the dominant discourses. The tale will be told not only through scholarly works, but also through literary and journalistic accounts, as well as ethnographic data I have gathered.

African History and Myths

Well before the arrival of mass media, the continent had been *invented* in texts written by outsiders. According to Valentin Y. Mudimbe,

> one can observe three complementary genres of "speeches" contributing to the invention of a primitive Africa: the exotic text on savages, represented by travelers' reports; the philosophical interpretations about a hierarchy of civilizations; and the anthropological search for primitiveness. The complementarity of these speeches is obvious. It is perceived as a unity in the Western consciousness. (1988, p. 69)

For a long period of time, Western imagination held that Africa was populated with *barbarians* (the *Berbers* lived in the *Barbaria* south of North Africa),[2] cannibals, and large-headed diminutive black men, in other words, beings different from Europeans. These conceptions underwent some change during the colonial expansion, which brought about an increase in exchanges between Europeans and Africans. In the eighteenth and nineteenth centuries, explorers who published chronicles of their travels in West Africa were often sent out and supported by scholarly societies, such as the Royal Geographic Society of London. One of the first to penetrate the West African interior, Mungo Park,[3] described the Africans he saw as savages, modeled on the "bons sauvages" theorized by Jean-Jacques Rousseau, the philosopher of the *Lumières* (Enlightenment). Park described his black travel companions as "these rude children of nature, free from restraint, [who] display their emotions in the strongest and the most expressive manner" (Park, 1830, p. 45). These early portrayals rendered Blacks not only as a group of largely indistinguishable humans, but also as less advanced than their European observers. Such descriptions created a notion of the "other" and reflected both the presumptions and sometimes the prejudices of the era. For today's reader they highlight the observers' inability to understand a society and culture exceedingly different from their own.

The military added yet another layer of definition to the ones the early explorers had created. They established the *régime d'exception*, also known as "colonialism," through the introduction of judicial, administrative, and tax structures; as such it grew out of a French notion of the nation-state. These European legislative and cultural concepts were entirely imposed. Missionaries and merchants accompanied them and were ultimately followed by civil servants and "experts," such as anthropologists in the 1940s and 1950s. Texts from the period reveal that each of these white "travelers" provided the colonial power with either material or symbolic means to better control the local peoples' attempts at maintaining their own sociocultural realities. Georges Balandier, the founder of the French school of Marxist anthropology, admits in the preface to his *Sociology of Black Africa* (first published in 1955) that he had been invited by the colonial administration to orient his own research

> to draw up a kind of balance sheet for two peoples . . . who attracted the attention
> of the administrative authorities by their enterprises and 'revival of initiative,' and
> now, after accepting the colonial situation for a time, were beginning to react against
> it by reorganizing themselves. (1970, p. 14)

Though Balandier and his followers over the years distanced themselves from the colonial enterprise, their attempt to describe the cultures they had witnessed were still grounded in French universalist ideals of "nationhood" which misrepresent the sociocultural situation of the Africans (Moore, 1994, pp. 99–104).

Even today, much writing on Africa perpetuates images that oversimplify the cultural diversity of the continent. Africans are depicted as members of a largely communal culture who lead traditional, unchanging or cyclical lives, diametrically opposed to those lived in the Western world. Institutionally, this point of view portrays Africans as "underdeveloped," once again at the bottom of a hierarchy culminating in Western forms of development considered as the apogee. Such reductionism overlooks the diversity and richness of the African world, as well as the fact that Africans have a history and they are our contemporaries; in other words, they inhabit the same universe as we do.

The first indigenous responses to Western ethnocentrism, the notions of "negritude" and "panafricanism," did not resolve the problem of the European reductionism of African realities. Although they restored the historical and political dimensions of the African setting, these theories were still based on universalist myths about the continent. For other thinkers of African origin, to justify cultural differences based on skin color or geographical location is to define culture extremely narrowly. If the premise that culture is lived and manifested at the interaction level is accepted (Giddens, 1984), communicational differences provide clear evidence of cultural diversity in Africa. The myth of an "africanness" spanning continents and oceans is certainly exactly that: a myth (Harris, 1992, p. 13). The African philosopher Kwame Anthony Appiah elaborates:

> Whatever Africans share, we do not have a common traditional culture, common languages, a common religious or conceptual vocabulary . . . we do not even belong to a common race; and since it is so, unanimism is not entitled to what is, in my view, its fundamental presupposition. . . . Africans share too many problems and projects to be distracted by a bogus basis for solidarity. (1992, pp. vii-ix)

Another way of negating African societies' diverse history is maintained by selective text use. Among the texts *neglected* by the majority of specialists are the almost 5000 Arab manuscripts of Gao and Tombouctou in Northern Mali, some of which can be dated back to the eleventh century. These texts, along with a great deal of other evidence, show that the history of West Africa is as long and eventful as that of the Western world (Fage, 1995; Iliffe, 1995; Ki-Zerbo, 1978). Just as the West has developed specific types of knowledge and technology, African cultures, nurturing a different experiential past, have developed different fields of knowledge and ideologies stressing different values. How much of this heritage remains today? In fact, a substantial amount, because European hegemony is relatively recent for most of West Africa, dating back no later than to the turn of the century. Africans today have retained a clear memory of the precolonial world, just as they have of the invasion and the colonial period which preceded independence (Bâ, 1991, 1994; Soyinka, 1972, 1983). Yet many texts about these periods are still relatively unknown.

As a social science professor from Benin succinctly states:

> Those who have had long-term contact with Africans or gave accurate accounts of what they observed were never heeded. Their theories were never accepted. Vast quantities of such chronicles and manuscripts authored by merchants or administrators have been lost or willfully ignored.[4]

A third type of exclusion of African societies' diverse situation is constructed through the nonrecognition of contemporaneity of Africans in written accounts, what the critical anthropologist Johannes Fabian calls "the denial of coevalness" (1983, p. 31). This notion refers to the need to situate Africans or "others" in the same time as ours and to recognize the fact that they are actors in the same world. Even if this is a lived experience of all those who have contacts with Africans, in the writing down of the ethnographic experience, "political space and political time [become] ideologically constructed instruments of power" (p. 144) that serve evolutionist views of civilizations. In such accounts, African societies are invariably placed at the bottom of the hierarchy in search of progress, modernity, and development.

African societies are different from, for example, Western societies. Yet today more than ever before, Africans live in a world becoming more interdependent and interconnected. Beyond the realities brought over by economic globalization, simple observation shows us that at the farthest corners of the West African savanna people listen to the same news on the radio as we do, watch Western movies at the *vidéo mobile,* and sometimes participate in television viewing. They also can travel and communicate with parents, friends, or colleagues across the globe, using telephone networks connected by satellite. Though on the margins of the global economy, African people are part of larger processes of social change that originate in the Western world but affect everyone.

French Media Transplanted

In francophone West Africa, major changes were introduced by the colonial system. The French army's invasion of West Africa between 1880 and 1900 caused considerable bloodshed. Military occupation, "pacification" and the establishment of the administration that ensued also saw periods of physical violence, including compulsory work.[5] This physical violence was coupled with symbolic violence against all those who were not "citizens" but "subjects" of the "République Française." One of the many to attest to these events is Amadou Hampâté Bâ, a distinguished francophone author from the Fulani culture who began his professional life as a public servant in the colonial administration. At the time, in his autobiography, *Oui mon commandant!,* he notes that "the lowest of Whites always came before the highest of Blacks . . ." (1994, p. 187).[6]

In this colonial context, the mass media of francophone West Africa were not born until the 1930s, much later than those of the neighboring anglophone countries including Gambia, Ghana, Liberia, Nigeria, and Sierra Leone, where independent newspapers were introduced and prospered as early as the turn of the century. For many decades, despite the presence of an educated elite, particularly in Senegal and Benin, the French government discouraged the formation of a local press through prohibitive taxes on paper and printing equipment, while at the same time encouraging the circulation of newspapers from the "métropole." Commercial newspapers controlled by French interests, such as the Groupe de Breteuil, however, were set up in major francophone cities, such as Dakar and Abidjan in the 1930s, for readership of French expatriates and African *assimilés*. The first important "indigenous" francophone publications, however, did not get underway until the 1950s. The two most influential of them, *La Condition Humaine* and *Afrique Noire*, saw the light of day in the decade preceding the independences. They were founded by Félix Houphouët-Boigny and Léopold Senghor who were members of the French parliament, and who later became "fathers of independence" of Ivory Coast and Senegal, respectively. It was in this context that the poet and writer Léopold Senghor created the "negritude" theory to emphasize the uniqueness of Black African culture (1964).

Freedom of expression was for long inequally distributed between France and its colonies. Though French thinkers began to criticize colonialism by the end of the 1920s (Londres, 1929),[7] in Africa itself, the great majority of French "subjects" were exposed to official French propaganda right up to independence in 1960. In territories with a high rate of illiteracy, where the press had a limited impact, radio was perceived as a powerful tool to reach the population. Both francophone and anglophone radio were initially devised as instruments of colonial policy to replicate the structures of the former *métropole*. In keeping with the British model of indirect rule and the BBC, radio in anglophone countries was designed as a public service, most often broadcast in local languages. In francophone countries, however, radio was modeled on the metropolitan framework of state monopoly. Broadcasting occurred in the French language with the goal of centralization and assimilation. Most importantly, broadcasting was an instrument used by the French authorities to oppose the stirring of independence until local governments took it over for their own purposes.

Radio Tam-Tam, the Neocolonial Media

In the newly independent French West African countries, the mass media, newspapers, radio, and later television were conceptualized and officially presented as "public services," but in practice functioned as relays for the local governments' official position. The francophone African countries' new leaders soon developed new nationalist discourses, reflecting the elite interest, to build independent states within the artificial borders created by colonialism. Subsequently, socioeconomic development discourses were introduced, and since the early 1990s, the subject of democratization has been highlighted. Foreign and international funding agencies have understandably encouraged these last two themes. Furthermore, the broadcasting systems remained beholden to the former *métropole* by the means of funding, technical support, and programming.[8]

In African media organizations, decolonization replaced French expatriates' supervision of Africans with a new type of bureaucracy administered by Westernized Africans who were now in charge.[9] Even today state supervision runs deepest in the strategic sector of communications and has a profound impact on journalism. National media have crippling constraints placed directly on them by the central power, often by the head of state or his closest associates. Such a set-up results in the media being run by a bloated bureaucracy handing out patronage encouraging reporting that supports the status quo. Official media frequently limit themselves to recounting the activities of state dignitaries and transmitting their *langue de bois,* a technocratic discourse virtually devoid of meaning. In local parlance, media which sing the praises of the heads of state are known as "radio tam-tam," named after a type of drum which sings the praise of the chief.[10]

In spite of the use of the media as propagandists for their respective governments, the use of force to control people was long prevalent in francophone West Africa because the persuasive effects of broadcasting seemed limited. The Nigerian Nobel Prize recipient Wole Soyinka recounts when radio first came to his town how the children sang about this strange box "who speaks without expecting a reply: Rediffusion, white man's lies" (1981, p. 108). After independence, management by the new local powers did not bolster public trust in the quality of the information carried by the media. Part of this distrust is explained by the fact that, up until very recently, all francophone African journalists were hired as public servants, whose loyalty was not to the public but to the interests of the single party's leaders who held the state power. Beyond that, however, many Africans feel that journalists are also people unlike themselves: mostly educated and trained in Europe, they have been labeled as *Blancs-noirs* by Bâ (1994, p. 187). As such, they are perceived as Whites by members of their communities. As persons, they have incorporated a cultural duality that is difficult to bear. They are torn between the necessity to behave like Whites, while at the same time longing to return to their community of origin.[11]

The first *Blancs-noirs* trained abroad as journalists went to Paris to the *Studio école* of the *Société de Rediffusion de la France d'Outremer* (Sorafom). A senior West African journalist describes it as an institution that maintained a policy of segregation between Whites and Blacks and was therefore "another one of those places for niggers only!" Later on, the *Centre d'étude des sciences et techniques de l'information* (Cesti) was founded in Dakar, Senegal, to train local journalists (Tudesq, 1992). Here the setting became more egalitarian with French and sometimes Canadian professionals transmitting professional practices and values similar to those of their Western peers.[12] Yet, the question remains: do West Africans practice their profession in the same way? Although it is relatively easy to transmit standardized abilities and skills to produce and process information for different types of media institutions, the journalist's trade extends well beyond its technical aspects. It also concerns the learning of different roles and values designed to keep reporting relatively free of bias.

For African journalists, many of these imported media models and professional practices may contradict their own cultural contexts and statuses as *Blancs-noirs* and the necessity to follow community practices. One example of this is the fact that African customs forbid a person to ask an elder direct questions, and maintain that the words of a chief are never questioned. An elder or chief could nonetheless be challenged indirectly in ways sometimes found in mass media or interpersonal networks.

Radio Trottoir: Indigenous Communication Networks

A wind of change, "the wind from the East" as Malians called it, blew through most countries of francophone West Africa in 1990, making private media possible. Numerous newspapers sprang up in each country that tend to model themselves after *Le Monde, Libération,* or *Le Canard enchaîné* from Paris. These newspapers however contain articles written in a different mode from that found in the Western press. For example, "Lettre pour Laye," a widely read weekly column published in the Friday edition of *L'Observateur* in Ouagadougou, the capital of Burkina Faso, invariably begins with the following warning:

> Tipoko l'Intrigante tells nothing of herself; she makes nothing up. Tipoko l'Intrigante is a non-being. She is neither good nor evil. She follows her intuition because "intuition is a woman's gift that allows her to be sure of something without being perfectly certain."[13]

In this column, a journalist using a pseudonym reports on the opinions of Tipoko, a somewhat witching character. The information given in the column is often credible, but does not follow standard journalistic practices. It rarely cites sources or verifies the information concerning public figures—the head of state excluded. It offers as well political commentaries on events such as battles for chiefdoms and witchcraft.

How can such practices be understood? A number of African communication scholars have shown growing interest in how Africans understand and use media messages as well as how alternative communication networks function. Frank Okwu Ugboajah (1985), a Nigerian university professor, gave the name "ora-media" to these networks which generally follow local communication patterns. These traditional or folk media are based on what I call *endogenous communication processes*. To situate these processes in their proper context, it should be noted that if *Blancs-noirs* journalists live a cultural duality, then Africans in general must also function in everyday life within two worlds simultaneously. Even though French is the official language, all Africans remain marked by their native languages as well as their family, ethnic, and socioethnic cultures.[14] While aspects of "official" life and relations with the administration, the school and foreigners are carried out in French, private life still often unfolds in another language. There are hundreds of these native languages in West Africa. Some are widely spoken, usually those of dominant ethnic groups or tradespeople, whereas others are in danger of disappearing. In such a setting, young Africans are made aware of the complexities of interpersonal communication at a very early age. These dual communicational and cultural realities co-exist and influence the use and understanding of Western technology and its models.

This coexistence of endogenous and foreign communication patterns parallels the findings of feminist scholars who have noted that members of a dominated group have access and pay attention not only to their own culture and practices, but also to those of the dominant group to negotiate daily life situations (Harding, 1991; Narayan, 1989).[15] A social scientist from Senegal, Emmanuel Seyni Ndione, describes in *Le don et le recours* (1994) how those living in the poor and lower middle-class areas of Dakar (Senegal) are perpetually negotiating with the members of the various interpersonal networks that make up the capital city. He shows that, for these people, such networks are resources and opportunities that contribute to the survival of the extended family unit. For some Africans, this extended family (often synonymous with socioethnic affiliation) can actually include several hundred loosely related people and their dependents.

These interpersonal networks not only redistribute resources and solidarity, but also function as underground information networks called *radio trottoir* (sidewalk radio). *Radio trottoir* is an alternative to the mass media in that it offers opportunities for criticism of high-ranking personalities that no other medium could carry without consequences. Where does this kind of information originate? The sources of *radio trottoir* stories are difficult to trace, but since they include intimate details, they must originate with members of the officials' entourage, usually servants, chauffeurs, merchants, or other subordinates. Consequently, the key players in *radio trottoir* are on the margin of power, and this very marginality offers the opportunity to fill what are perceived as gaps in the official information channels.

Yet another more recent use of those networks is found among those journalists who are employed by the new private media, outside the official set up. For independent journalists, official information outlets (presidential and ministerial information services, local press agencies and organized media events) are not considered credible, except to document official changes of position. The essence of their work lies in developing alternative information sources to crosscheck the official information and situate it in its proper context. As one journalist said, "We spend a great deal of time 'making the rounds'" and conversing with members of various local networks. Often such get-togethers are held in bars, playgrounds, at informal meetings, or family events. In short, these journalists make it their business to be in contact with the sources of the latest *radio trottoir* news and those who interpret it. These new meeting-places can be seen as the modern equivalent of such ancient ones as the marketplace, the well, the palaver tree, and others. West African independent journalists more or less employ the same techniques as any competent investigative journalist, but more importantly, they have adapted them to the local communicative scene.

In West Africa as elsewhere on the continent, local networks complement the other mass media as information distributors. A case in point was the resignation of the prime minister of Mali on February 2, 1994, in the capital city of Bamako. Official television waited a full day before announcing this news, though most Malians knew about the event a few hours later through foreign radio broadcasts. What was also quickly learned through *radio trottoir* was that the information delay by the official media stemmed from the fact that the head of state was trying to convince the prime minister to reconsider his decision. Leaked by members of the president's entourage, this information traveled throughout Mali by word-of-mouth and telephone until it reached the far corners of the land (Péricard, 1995).

Mass Media and Endogenous Communication Networks

To complete the discussion of communication processes in francophone West Africa, it is necessary to give a short account of listeners and viewers and their idiosyncrasies. At present, unfortunately, few African audience studies exist. Many of the ones that are available furthermore have been commissioned by Western funding agencies and are therefore relatively narrowly focused.[16] However, evidence gathered in the field clearly shows that African audiences are highly diversified and unpredictable. It is well known that print reaches only a minority of the population. Radio and television are accessible to the majority of those who understand French.[17] Each audience group follows different reading, listening, viewing, and interpretive strategies.

With regard to the news, *Blancs-noirs*, the educated Africans, constitute an important link in the information distribution processes. They select pertinent information tid-bits from a variety of sources, discuss it among themselves and then re-direct it to the members of their own network. These individuals add relevant context not supplied by the media. For example, certain international issues are of interest to the majority of Africans in a context where only a minority of the population have studied the French language used by most of the media.[18] Such information provides insight into the intentions of relevant Western countries, France in particular, with respect to issues of economic support and political cooperation. Moreover, French-language international radio broadcasts which carry news by short-wave are considered more credible than the official media and thus complement them. A senior executive in Burkina Faso told me:

> I prefer to deprive myself of food than of information. At 4:30 am, I listen to RFI [Radio France Internationale], and the BBC [British Broadcasting Corporation]. At 5:30, it is RFI once again and the Voice of America. At 6:30, I tune in to Radio Burkina and RFI once more. I then discuss all I have heard with my family, friends, and colleagues. My understanding of a problem may not be the same as that of another and, as we say, it is discussion that sheds light on matters. It is crucial to know if there is any additional information that one or the other possesses.[19]

In the extended family, such information can be used to establish and maintain ties with crucial external networks within a country public service as well as with members of international aid organizations. Depending on the ethnic group, complex negotiation processes allow collective strategies to be developed and implemented.[20] Elders and chiefs function as mediators in the process of establishing consensus within their community. Decisions arrived at through long deliberation (the palaver), are not conveyed by the chiefs themselves, but by their designated spokesperson, the *griot*. A similar practice of information dissemination is found as well on the government level where designated journalists or media figures are known to have insight into the positions of the head of state.[21] If such a source begins to criticize an official personality, it is understood that this individual's replacement is likely, giving those who may be affected by this decision the chance to adapt their strategies.

Media messages are used differently by the less educated milieus. In areas surrounding large African cities, where cultural intermixing is common, having a multiplicity of information sources may be necessary for the survival of both the individual and the marginals' solidarity networks whose members exchange relevant intelligence. New popular culture productions also generate communitarian experiences in these suburban zones. Ratings in urban areas reveal the vast popularity of foreign television products, such as weekly series, movies, and sporting events. Local television stations also re-broadcast music and dance clips, which are extremely popular, as are documentaries. Programs broadcast in major local languages are most often educational, therefore less interesting. Certain showcase events, such as the traditional wrestling games in Niger where TV reaches a remarkable 80 percent of residents, bring administration and commerce to a standstill. Local productions nonetheless remain affected by the shortage of resources thus only adding to the administrative sluggishness.

Although the number of television sets is relatively low, between one in a thousand citizens and one in twenty in exceptional francophone African countries, group viewing practices expose virtually the entire population of urban areas to certain television shows. In Mali, *Dynasty* (Spelling, 1981–1989) made Alexis clothing fashionable and caused a drastic increase in the number of children named Christelle or Blake. But an official from the Malian Television and Radio Broadcasting Office (ORTM) cautioned this did not mean that the world represented in *Dynasty* was considered acceptable. Instead, the fascination of the series lies in the depiction of corruption in a perceived global power center like the United States.[22] Though the material accessories of *Dynasty* may seduce the viewing audience, this does not imply that the values conveyed by the series are accepted. Rather, images from *Dynasty* or *Dallas* (Brown, 1978–1991) convey, no matter how distorted they are, how power in the Western capitalist business world works. To those who are on the margins of global society, these images may offer pertinent information about the globalization of trade relations.

What is the situation for the more isolated villages, where close to 70 or 80 percent of the population live? Here generator-powered *vidéo mobiles* occasionally offer Western or Asian movies for 100 to 150 francs CFA (between 20 and 30 American cents). These villages are furthermore served by radio. However, essential information is still primarily transmitted through the informal channel of *radio trottoir* or, more precisely by the *téléphone de brousse* (bush telephone) as it is called in the rural context. This figurative grapevine can actually be constituted by telephone as well as by travelers, especially youths and female merchants. Their activities bring them into contact with networks in the major cities of the area. Though this mobility is at first sight physical, on the communicational level it spans diverse levels of culture and power. Some female merchants may have several places of residence and speak up to a dozen local languages in addition to English and French. A substantial number of marginalized educated youths also travel from place to place, getting to know the associated milieu and sometimes even crossing the continent to France. In the process, they create vast exchange and negotiation networks whose benefits are felt both collectively and individually.

French Universalism and Cultural Relativism

In addition to the physical, military, administrative, and political result of colonialism, francophone West Africa has experienced other more subtle forms
of domination imposed by French intellectuals. This domination is manifested
in how the French media disperse information about the region. It has, as we
have seen, led to the creation of alternative information channels among West
Africans, to supplement metropolitan and official information sources. Furthermore, the African populations have maintained and developed their own
networks such as *radio trottoir* to react against the messages and images diffused
through the media. The rerouting of media information by Africans within their
indigenous communication networks also attests to forms of resistance local
cultures have developed vis-à-vis the postindustrial West and the Westernized
national authorities.

Whether two such different cultural forms can coexist has been widely debated not only in scholarly circles but also in the popular press, where cultural
relativism seems to have become a politically correct stance in English-speaking countries. Yet, in French intellectual circles, so-called cultural relativism is
frowned upon as retrograde and racist. In trying to understand this polarization
one might ask whether the refusal of many French intellectuals to recognize
separate African identities amounts to an attempt to legitimate a universalist
and republican tradition which reaches back to the Enlightenment, and to use
this tradition for hegemonic purposes. The result has been that, while doing so,
they have constructed their own culture as the norm and hierarchized the others'
cultures, including those from Africa, as inferior to it. The Beninese philosopher
Paulin Hountondji (1977, p. 219) observes that there are three distinct aspects to
what is implied in the notion of "cultural plurality." First, it refers to the multitude
of cultures which are found in a given geographical region. Second, it implies
the recognition of this plurality by those who write about these cultures. And
third, it may entail the value judgment that plurality should be encouraged. The
experiences of ethnographers, of travelers, and of Africans themselves document
the singularity and complexity of African cultures. As Appiah (1992) points
out, it is not so much the recognition of difference that constitutes the basis of
racism, as it is the theory of evolution, which stratifies cultures on the basis of
Western universalist criteria, particularly those coming from the tradition of
the Enlightenment. Rejecting these well-documented evidences amounts to an
ideological stance on the part of some French intellectuals.

In the context of the francophone West African mass media, the media
system helps impose the allegedly universal French and Western definitions of
given situations, to which certain practices of journalists and audiences respond
by the use of endogenous communication processes as a means of resistance.

This observation shows that the recognition of cultural factors is more than a condition necessary for the media to meet the needs of the citizens of francophone West Africa. It is also a condition that must be met before a dialogue between Africans and Westerners may become possible.

NOTES

1. The most important institution common to the countries of francophone Western Africa the *Union monétaire et économique ouest-africaine* (West-African Economic and Monetary Union). This monetary union has the *Banque centrale des Etats d'Afrique de l'Ouest* (States of Western Africa Central Bank) as a governing body seeing to matters concerning the common currency, the Franc CFA (Franc de la *Communauté financière africaine*). Since the Bank of France guarantees the convertibility of the Franc CFA, its policies carry considerable weight when dealing with the region's monetary issues. Among the nine countries of francophone Western Africa, only Mauritania is relatively financially independent of the former colonial power after creating its own currency, the ouguiya.

2. Ancient maps of Africa show that the continent's interior was virtually unknown to Europeans up until the end of the eighteenth or beginning of the nineteenth century (Allen, 1992), despite the awareness of highly detailed Arabic chronicles for many centuries. European geographers had the *Barbaria* begin south of North Africa. The *Nigrita* was a vast territory covering all of the Sudanese savanna from what is now known as Senegal all the way to Ethiopia.

3. Mungo Park made his way through Gambia between 1795 and 1797 until he arrived downstream from Ségou in modern-day Mali, after which he published *Travels in the Interior of Africa*. One of his best-known successors was René Caillé, whose work *Le journal d'un voyageur*(1830) created a considerable stir in France. Another major explorer was German scholar Heinrich Barth. In 1858 he published *Travels and Discoveries in North and Central Africa*, the first serious study of the human and physical aspects of the territory which later became northern Mali and Niger.

4. Interview with Marcel Missigbeto (biologist and economist) in Niamey, Niger, January 17, 1994.

5. The atrocities committed in Africa by the French colonialists were never thoroughly documented, let alone acknowledged and compensated for (Brunschwig, 1988; Pacéré, 1979). This means that Africans today live with the silent memories of the colonial horrors and injustices; injustices carried out by conquerors for whom there could never be tribunals like those held in Nuremberg or The Hague.

6. "Le dernier des Blancs venait toujours avant le premier des Noirs."

7. After a visit to what is now known as francophone Western Africa in 1929, journalist Albert Londres published *Terre d'ébène (La traite des Noirs)*. He denounced the practices of public servants, members of the clergy and merchants, and also gave detailed accounts of the violence, high-handed conduct, and contempt that characterized the colonial system. He drew the conclusion that the treatment of Blacks in the colonies amounted to a form of slavery. This was understandably quite a shock for the French public, who until then perceived colonialism as a *civilizing mission* with the intent of improving the quality of life for Africans. This publication instigated the first protests against the colonial system in the press and the French parliament. As a result, many intellectuals and part of France's left-wing press became associated with the anticolonial movement.

8. Independence of African states did not reduce Western presence. There are more expatriates from the West living in Africa today than there were colonialists prior to independence

(Hancock, 1991). Although their political clout has waned, Westerners have held on to enormous power by dividing up and administering the budgets of the foreign aid which, in some countries, represents 20 percent of the gross domestic product or the equivalent to two-thirds of the state budget.

9. This is what a farmer from Senegal implied when he declared: "Independence is great, but when does it end?"

10. The drums used by many West-African ethnic groups make it possible to transmit detailed messages in the form of metaphors and parables over long distances. Among other ethnic groups, this technique is used by the Mosse of Burkina Faso and the Baoule of the Ivory Coast (Pacéré, 1991; Bouah, 1989). Different drums transmit different types of messages, sometimes right across a kingdom by means of a relay system.

11. The cultural duality lived by *Blancs-noirs* is characterized by tension between *mimesis* and *nostalgia*. *Mimesis*, which means being and acting like a White person, is the result of history and Western training that proposes Western ideals, yet keeps educated Africans cut-off from the West (Memmi, 1965; Bhabha, 1994). *Nostalgia* is an unachievable desire to return to the warmth of the community which takes root while studying far away from one's family.

12. Upon completion of their studies, CESTI graduated are placed with media in France or French Canada to gain work experience. Overall, the Westerners feel that these budding African journalists are professionals with the same qualifications as their counterparts trained in France or Canada.

13. "Tipoko l'Intrigante n'apprend rien d'elle-même, elle n'invente jamais rien. Tipoko l'Intrigante est un non être. Elle n'est ni bonne en elle-même, ni mauvaise en elle-même. Elle fonctionne par intuition, car 'l'intuition c'est la faculté qu'a une femme d'être sûre d'une chose sans en avoir la certitude . . . .'"

14. Identity in Africa is generally based on gender, age group (where children are usually raised by an aunt or uncle) and ethnicity (characterized by language and a specific social organization) as well as socioethnic affiliation. This last criterion comes from the distinction made between the various categories of families: chiefs, blacksmiths, merchants, former slaves, *griots* (genealogists, musicians, and spokespeople), or others.

15. According to Uma Narayan, a philosopher from India, "groups, whether women, the poor or racial minorities may derive an 'epistemic advantage' from having knowledge of the practices of both their own contexts and those of their oppressors. The practices of the dominant group (for instance, men) govern a society; the dominated group (for instance, women) must acquire some fluency with these practices in order to survive in that society" (1989, p.265).

16. A few years ago, an international organization searched for a solution to the following problem: TV viewers in Mauritania reacted negatively to commercials. They believed that a product that needed to be publicly lauded was unworthy of their attention. The research carried out did not focus on the underlying causes of the problem. Ample evidence shows that publicity is not always as effective as advertisers claim it to be, especially in non-Western cultures. In this instance, research focused instead on how to present publicity to TV viewers and announcers most convincingly. It was more marketing than actual research.

17. It should be noted that more and more radio programs presented in local languages are produced in francophone West Africa, particularly in rural areas where a growing number of community radio stations, usually financed by international or foreign organizations, are operating.

18. In francophone West Africa, French is more often learned at school. But according to offical statistics, the countries of francophone West Africa have the following rates of illiteracy:

Niger	86.4%
Burkina Faso	80.8%
Mali	69%
Senegal	66.9%
Guinea	64.1%
Benin	63%
Mauritania	62.3%
Ivory Coast	59.9%
Togo	48.3%

19. Interview with Arona Sy (sociologist) in Ouagadougou, Burkina Faso, July 2, 1993.

20. These strategies generally strive for political and economic objectives by establishing ties with external networks. Ever since the beginning of colonialism, certain groups have had some of their young taught to understand how administration works and establish networks within the public service. I observed such activity among the Wolof of Senegal, the Mosse of Burkina Faso, and the Baoule of the Ivory Coast. It was also observed in outlying ethnic groups, such as the Songhay of Mali and the Zarma of Niger. Collective strategies are clearly based on a communicational and intercultural competence shared by the diverse groups of a single community. Decisions are made on the basis of opinions expressed not only by the educated and those in positions of authority, but also marginal groups such as women and youths.

21. Similar sources of privileged information are also found in the European opinion press. They only have a minority following, however.

22. Interview with Tiemoko Macalou, director of the second radio broadcasting channel, in Bamako, Mali, February 25, 1994.

REFERENCES

Allen, P. (1992). *The Atlas of Atlases: The Map Maker's Vision of the World*. London: Marshall.

Appiah, K. A. (1992). *In My Father's House: Africa in the Philosophy of Culture*. New York: Oxford University Press.

Bâ, A.H. (1991). *Amkoullel, l'enfant peul: Mémoires*. Arles: Actes Sud.

Bâ, A.H. (1994). *Oui mon commandant! Mémoires. T.2*. Arles: Actes Sud.

Balandier, G. (1970). *The Sociology of Black Africa: Social Dynamics in Central Africa*. New York: Oxford University Press.

Barth, H. (1857). *Travel and Discoveries in North and Central Africa*. New York: Harper.

Bhabha, H.K. (1994). *The Location of Culture*. New York: Routledge.

Bouah, N. (1989). "Tambours parleurs en Côte d'Ivoire." In *Corps sculptés, corps parés, corps masqués: Chefs-d'oeuvre de Côte d'Ivoire*. Paris:Galeries Nationales du Grand Palais.

Bourgault, L.M. (1995). *Mass Media in Sub-Saharan Africa*. Bloomington: Indiana University Press.

Brown, J.H. (Producer). (1978-1991). *Dallas*. New York: CBS.

Brunschwig, H. (1988). *L'Afrique noire au temps de l'empire français*. Paris: Denoël.

Caillé, R. (1830). *Travels through Central Africa to Timbuctoo*. London: Colburn & Bentley.

Fabian, J. (1983). *Time and the Other: How Anthropology Makes Its Object*. New York: Columbia University Press.

Fage, J. D. (1995). *A History of Africa*. New York: Routledge.

Giddens, A. (1984). *The Constitution of Society*. Berkeley: University of California Press.

Hancock, G. (1991). *Lords of Poverty: The Power, Prestige, and Corruption of the International Aid Business*. New York: Atlantic Monthly Press.

Harding, S. (1991). *Whose Science? Whose Knowledge? Thinking from Women's Lives*. Ithaca: Cornell University Press.

Harris, E. L. (1992). *Native Stranger: A Black American's Journey into the Heart of Africa*. New York: Vintage Books.

Hountondji, P. J. (1977). *Sur la philosophie africaine: Critique de l'ethnophilosophie*. Paris: Maspéro.

Iliffe, J. (1995). *Africans: The History of a Continent*. Cambridge: Cambridge University Press.

Ki-Zerbo, J. (1978). *Histoire de l'Afrique noire: D'hier à demain*. Paris: Hatier.

Londres, A. (1929). *Terre d'ébène (La traite des Noirs)*. Paris: Albin Michel.

Memmi, A. (1965). *The Colonizer and the Colonized*. Boston: Beacon Press.

Moore, S. F. (1994). *Anthropology and Africa: Changing Perspectives on a Changing Scene*. Charlottesville: University Press of Virginia.

Mudimbe, V. Y. (1988). *The Invention of Africa: Gnosis, Philosophy,andtheOrderofKnowledge*. Bloomington: Indiana University Press.

Narayan, U. (1989). "The Project of Feminist Epistemology: Perspectives from a Nonwestern Feminist." In A. M. Jaggar and S. R. Bordo (Eds.) *Gender/Body/Knowledge: Feminist Reconstructions of Being and Knowing* (pp. 256-269). New Brunswick: Rutgers University Press.

Ndione, E. S. (1994). *L'économie urbaine en Afrique: Le don et le recours*. Paris: Karthala; Dakar; Enda Graf.

Pacéré, T. F. (1979). *Ainsi on a assassiné tous les Mossé*. Sherbrooke, Naaman.

Pacéré, T. F. (1991). *Le langage des tam-tams et des masques en Afrique (bendrologie): Une littérature méconnue*. Paris: L'Harmattan.

Park, M. (1830). *Travels in the Interior of Africa*. Edinburgh: William P. Nimmo.

Péricard, A. (1995). "Mali." In G. Hennebelle (Ed.), *Les télévisions du monde* (pp. 348-359). Paris: Corley.

Senghor, L. C. (1964). *Liberté I: Négritude et humanisme*. Paris: Seuil.

Soyinka, W. (1972). *The Man Died: Prison Notes of Wole Soyinka*. New York: Harper & Row.

Soyinka, W. (1981). *Aké, the Years of Childhood*. London: Arrow Books.

Spelling, A. (Producer). (1981–1989). *Dynasty*. New York: ABC.

Tudesq, A.-J. (1992). *L'Afrique noire et ses télévisions*. Paris: Anthropos/INA.

Ugboajah, F. O. (Ed.). (1985). *Mass Communication, Culture and Society in West Africa*. New York: Hans Zell.

DISCUSSION QUESTIONS

1. How has the colonial invasion been legitimated in Europe?

2. How has Africa been "invented" through narratives? Who were the key authors of and actors in this "invention" of the black continent? What are the consequences in the way Westerners perceive Africa today? What could be the conditions for a better understanding of African cultures and African people?

3. What do terms like "tribal," "primitive," "savage," "traditional," and "underdeveloped" have in common when applied to African people? To which social theories or concepts are they related? What is the French contribution to the creation of these notions?

4. How can we compare African and Western cultures? What are the components of different cultures that could be compared? What similarities, if any, do you notice between African and African-American cultures?

5. What were the main similarities and differences between the French and the British colonial systems in West Africa as evidenced in their use of the mass media?

6. What have been the four major periods in the past century leading to modern day West Africa?

7. Who were the major actors in the independence of francophone West African countries? In what ways have their theories and practices created new problems during the postcolonial period?

8. In what sense can one say that francophone West Africa is only marginally francophone?

9. What is the role of the French language, culture, and institutions in this part of the world? How have the colonial policies shaped the media systems in francophone West Africa?

10. How do the different groups of West African people use the messages of the mass media? What are the main differences between African and Western audiences?

11. What are endogenous communication networks? Who are the key actors in these networks and what are their strategies?

12. How can feminist theory help us to understand the actual situations of some social groups in francophone West Africa? What do women in the West and the poor or marginalized in Africa have in common?

13. What are the forces and the limits of both universalistic and relativistic positions when applied to the study of African situations and cultures?

14. How are globalization processes introducing new changes in francophone West Africa?

CHAPTER TWO

Tradition, Modernity, and the Clash of Cultures in African Society: The Example of Burkina Faso

Paschal B. Kyiiripuo Kyoore

African society has experienced tremendous social, economic, political, and cultural transformations since its first contact with Western society. As students of African history know very well, this contact was the result of a hegemonic enterprise undertaken by European countries on the continent. The European colonial enterprise in Africa gave birth to the modern states of Africa as we know them today. However, colonialism did not just create states. It also affected the cultures of the people living there. European systems often replaced African ones, thus imposing new political modes. The educational systems were also transformed to conform to the European worldview and to fulfill the goals of the colonial powers. Inevitably, this phenomenon has had an effect on African traditions and customs, thus provoking a clash between tradition and so-called modernity. Modernity here does not mean an exclusive European contribution to the world order. Rather, it is often the European element of "modernity" that clashes with traditional African modes of thought. Society in Burkina Faso has continuously been confronted with otherness. This otherness was a reality in the colonial era, and it has been transformed into new dimensions in contemporary society. As Richard Bjornson has observed specifically about African society, when confronted with otherness, people are obliged to reflect upon their own identity. Nineteenth-century European imperialism thrust Africans, and among them the people of Burkina Faso, into just such a confrontation (8–9).

Consequences of French Colonial Policies and Ideologies

The notion of a conflict of cultures in the former French colony of Burkina Faso—known as Upper Volta during the colonial era—is to be examined here. It was at the Berlin Conference of 1884 that European countries engaged in the colonial enterprise in Africa partitioned the continent into the countries as we know them today. Upper Volta became a colony of France in 1896. It gained independence from France in 1960 when most African countries under French colonial domination also gained their independence. The country changed its name to Burkina Faso in 1984 when the late Captain Thomas Sankara was president. The name Burkina Faso reflects the multilingual and multi-ethnic nature of the country. "Burkina" in the Mooré language means the dignity and the cultural patrimony of the people of the nation. "Faso" in the Dioula language means "my father's house." "Burkinabé" is the name of the nationality of the people. It is a Peul word, which means "people." Burkina Faso has had a succession of governments and heads of states as follows: 1960–1966 under Maurice Yaméogo; 1966–1980 under Sangoulé Lamizana; 1980–1982 under Saye Zerbo; 1982–1983 under Jean-Bapiste Ouédraogo; 1983–1987 under Thomas Sankara; and 1987–present under Blaise Compaoré.

The so-called civilizing mission of France had as its goal the deculturation of Africans. It was meant to distance Africans from their own culture and hence to inculcate in them a sense of inferiority vis-à-vis Western culture. Africans were educated in French established schools to internalize the values of French society and to develop an infatuation for everything French. This attempt to impose French culture on the people of Upper Volta resulted, inevitably, in a conflict of worldviews between the dominator and the dominated (the colonizer and the colonized).

Inherent in this ongoing clash of Western and African cultures is a conflict of generations. The younger generation of today is exposed to Western culture in a way that the generation of their parents was not. The older generation lived under colonial rule but did not attend the colonial schools. Generational conflicts are bound to occur in any culture, because the younger generation usually has not had the same experiences in life as the older one. Consequently, they might react differently in different circumstances. In the African experience with colonialism, however, the generational differences today are sharpened because of the opportunities that Western education and imported Western technology have made available to people of the younger generation.

In Burkina Faso, as is the case in other African countries, knowledge of a European language means access to certain privileges that are denied to the illiterate population. Good employment in the urban areas is more accessible to people with formal French education. Naturally, this can create generational conflicts when people of the older generation, who feel they should be more respected in society, are denied access to high-paying jobs because of their lack of the requisite diplomas.

The introduction of French education in Burkina Faso has resulted in a reassessment of what qualified skills are. The older generation also has limited access to some of the advantages of modern technology, not only because they cannot afford it, but also because they would not be able to enjoy the full benefits of such new technology. Consequently, there is the feeling among people of the older generation, and rightly so, that Western education and Western technology have widened the social, political, and economic gap between them and the younger generation. Access to Western education generates economic and political power. So, contact with Western culture in Burkina Faso has not just caused a conflict of cultures, but also generational conflicts that stem from differences in access to social, economic, and political power.

The tension between tradition and modernity can be explained partly as a consequence of the impossibility of reconciling two cultures that do not necessarily share the same values. In order to comprehend fully the nature of this tension, it is crucial to understand how much destruction was wrought on traditional African sociopolitical systems by the French colonial enterprise in Burkina Faso.[1]

One of the most profound transformations that European colonialism brought about in Africa was the creation of a new elite different from the traditional one and often in conflict with it. This new elite was formed through a French educational system that sought to foster a sense of inferiority about the Africans' own traditions and customs. The anthropologist Melville Herskovits has observed in a study on colonization in Africa that habits change faster than concepts under the weight of pressure from foreign cultures. Under such conditions, he argues, people often tend to maintain the old value systems and do not break completely from their customs (180–181). It is this type of cultural mutation that Burkinabé society has witnessed.

The brutal irruption of French economic values served to create a veritable alienation of the new African elite from traditions normally instilled by the family. (The crucial question now is whether or not Burkinabé or any other society can borrow the technology of another without simultaneously adopting, at least in part, its ideology.) Technology typically comes with an ideology and a way of life. Consequently, the new elite in Burkinabé society has forged for itself a lifestyle that corresponds to new tastes and habits. Furthermore, consumption of goods imported from the West also implies the adaptation of certain perceptions of human relationships that do not necessarily tally with the African worldview. Moreover, young Burkinabé citizens who have been directly exposed to the French system of education face the additional challenge of reconciling two different worlds. Those who cannot find equilibrium between the two value systems find themselves between two worlds.

French colonial schools in Africa were established to fulfill a political as well as a social function (Gadjigo 54). This goal is manifest in the words of Georges Hardy, a French colonial administrator in Africa:

> Pour transformer les peuples primitifs de nos colonies, pour les rendre le plus possible dévoués à notre cause et utiles à notre entreprise, nous n'avons à notre disposition qu'un nombre très limité de moyens et le moyen le plus sûr, c'est de prendre l'indigène dès l'enfance, d'obtenir de lui qu'il nous fréquente assidûment et qu'il subisse nos habitudes intellectuelles et morales (qtd. in Gadjigo 54).[2]

[In order to change the primitive people of our colonies, in order to make them most devoted to our cause and useful to our enterprise, we have at our disposal only a limited number of means, and the most certain means is to take the indigenous person right from childhood, to make him keep company with us faithfully and be subjected to our intellectual and moral habits].

To a large extent, this French colonial policy that George Hardy expresses so succinctly was successful. It was through the educational system that France was able to subject Africans in its colonies to its intellectual and moral habits. To be able to advance in the new educational system, young Burkinabé citizens had to attend school in one of the large urban areas at some point in their life. Obviously, this phenomenon had a tremendous social and cultural impact on them and the rest of the society. They developed certain habits and tastes, which came with French cultural indoctrination.

Migration into the urban areas is one of the phenomena that resulted from the quest to satisfy new tastes created by the importation of foreign goods. The urban areas are attractive to young people who hope to find jobs that are not available in the rural areas. This quest often leads young Burkinabé citizens to migrate not only to large urban areas like Bobo Dioulasso and Ouagadougou but also into neighboring countries such as Côte d'Ivoire and Ghana. Migration into urban areas leads to the temporary loss of direct contact with one's immediate family. This lack of interaction with one's family has enormous social and psychological consequences for the entire society. Urban dwellings thus become the space for a potential conflict of cultures. Migrant workers are faced with the challenge of finding a balance between the world of the village and that of the city, which tends to be heavily influenced by Western culture.

Every society evolves in one way or another, irrespective of whether or not there is any influence from outside cultures, although it would be hard to find a society that has not borrowed from or had imposed upon it certain elements from other cultures.

The vestiges of French colonial rule in Africa continue to be evident in every aspect of the lives of people from the countries it colonized, even years after they received their nominal independence. Critics have argued that the use of the term *postcolonial* might in itself be a misnomer. No matter whether the phenomenon in question is referred to as postcolonialism or neocolonialism, we are basically dealing with the issue of how Africans strive to find an equilibrium (in social, political, and cultural terms) between a foreign culture and their own.

One African nationalist who wrote about the importance of cultural identity in the fight against colonialism and imperialism was Amilcar Cabral. He was from Guinea- Bissau and was the founder and Secretary-General of the Partido Africano da Independencia da Guiné e Cabo Verde (PAIGC). He fought

Portuguese and generally European imperialism in his country when it was still under Portuguese colonial domination. He believed strongly in the need for Africans and other colonized peoples to fight against not just political but also cultural imperialism. For him, cultural identity went hand in hand with political freedom. Cabral "read" culture as the epistemology of geo-political relations within a society or between different societies. Epistemology is the theory of knowledge especially with regard to its methods and validation.

Cabral's theories of cultural domination are relevant to the present discussion of the conflict of cultures in Burkina Faso, a country that was colonized by the French. Cabral sees the value of culture as a factor of resistance to foreign domination. He argues that history teaches us that whatever may be the material aspect of foreign domination, it can be maintained only by the permanent, organized repression of the cultural life of the people concerned (Cabral 53). French assimilationist policies in Africa in general and in Burkina Faso in particular were forged to maintain an organized repression of the cultural life of the people. The question that now needs to be asked is how well the Burkinabé people have resisted the continual domination of Western culture many years after they gained their political independence from France. The issue of a conflict of generations and a conflict of cultures is directly related to this dilemma, a dilemma that is common to all African countries.

Cabral said of European colonial assimilationist ideology that the failure in its implementation was proof of its lack of viability and of its inhuman character. He writes:

> Culture is always in the life of a society . . . the more or less conscious result of the economic and political activities of that society, the more or less dynamic expression of the kinds of relationships which prevail in that society, on the one hand between man . . . and nature, and, on the other hand, among individuals, groups of individuals, social strata or classes. (54)

In Burkina Faso, the economic and political activities of society are more or less the conscious result of how society has dealt with the issue of contact with Western and more specifically French culture. Contemporary Burkinabé society has to cope with how to preserve the various cultures of its people against the onslaught of Western value systems. Very often these value systems are consumed uncritically by people too eager to assimilate foreign cultures at the expense of losing respect for the values of their own culture. Like most other African countries, Burkina Faso is very much economically dependent on other countries to provide goods and services that it cannot provide itself. This dependency has led to the problem of an uncritical consumption of Western values in both the cultural and economic sense.

Cabral has further observed in the light of colonial experience and cultural assimilation that the colonizer has not only created a system to repress the cultural life of the colonized people but has also provoked and developed the cultural alienation of a part of the population. Colonization created a social gap between the indigenous elites and the popular masses. Consequently, considerable parts of the population, notably the urban and rural petite bourgeoisie, have assimilated the mentality of the colonizer and now consider themselves culturally superior to their own people and ignore or look down upon traditional values (Cabral 57). These observations are pertinent to the experience of Burkinabé society. The clash of cultures in Burkina Faso has not only arisen because of the great impact that French culture has had on the elite, but also because French culture has filtered through every aspect of people's lives. Moreover, the rural dwellers just like the urban people are directly affected by the global economic scene, which is controlled by multinational companies in the West. In turn, the way they perceive their own culture is greatly influenced by such direct contact with French and generally Western worldviews in the political, social, and cultural arenas.

Assimilation as a French Political Strategy

It is crucial to understand the history and the philosophy behind French assimilationist policies in Africa in order to appreciate the profundity of the problem. According to Raymond Betts who has written on this phenomenon, there were two important elements underlying the doctrine of assimilation: the idea of basic human equality and the value of education as a corrective to environmental differences. French people had a tendency to think that all humanity should think and feel the way they did. This chauvinistic attitude gave way to proselytism in French national spirit (Betts 25). French assimilationist ideology was reinforced through their so-called *mission civilisatrice*. This ideology was justified in their view by what they considered to be the moral duty of the conqueror toward the conquered.

France wanted to integrate the people of its colonies culturally and politically. As Michael Crowder recalls, its assimilationist policy was based on the revolutionary doctrine of the equality of all peoples and at the same time on the assumption of the superiority of European and, in particular, French civilization (Crowder 1–2). Thus, according to Crowder, the French had a fundamental acceptance of the Africans' potential human equality, but totally dismissed the value of African culture (2). This attitude obviously created a paradox. The French mentality justified colonization in countries such as Burkina Faso, and since there was no respect for the culture of the people, the emphasis in the school curriculum was on European history and French literature and culture. Since then, some of its own postcolonial governments have made efforts to instill a sense of authenticity in Burkinabé society, but with different levels of success.

As is the case in other African countries, Burkinabé society has reacted in diverse forms to this colonial heritage at different times in its history. As Richard Bjornson has succinctly observed, "the assimilation of European culture implied a renunciation of traditional African values, but many of these values continued to serve educated Africans as primary points of reference in their universe of discourse" (19). In Burkina Faso, this phenomenon has manifested itself in the types of governments that the country has had since its independence in 1960 and also in the type of elite that controls the economic and political life of the people. Again, Bjornson is right in arguing that despite the ambiguous position of the European-educated African torn between two cultures, European culture left an indelible imprint on the African mentality. In fact, many Africans developed a strong sense of allegiance to it.

Literary Representations of the Conflict of Cultures

Neocolonialism in the form of global economic and political control has made Burkinabé society particularly vulnerable to the manipulation of Western powers in the context of people's attempts to maintain their cultural and political identity. Some Burkinabé intellectuals, products of the educational system that contemporary society inherited from the former colonizers, have found various forms of literary expression through which they address this phenomenon. One of those literary modes is drama. As a result, the theater offers plays inspired by the daily mutations of society in its bid to come to terms with what some call modernity. Furthermore, the theater can reach a large portion of the population including the illiterate class.

Traditional versus Modern Practices and Values

One Burkinabé playwright is Jean-Pierre Guingané. In his play *Papa Oublie-Moi*, he evokes issues directly related to the welfare of children. In the traditional society, the responsibility for bringing up children is the duty of the society at large—thus the popular African saying that it takes a village to raise a child. Nonetheless, this concept does not suggest that society does not expect parents of children to play their natural role as the primary educators of their children, and what Guingané depicts in his play is the irresponsible behavior of a parent who reneges on his responsibility toward his children. While traditional society often tended to impose too much responsibility for raising children on mothers alone, society still expected fathers to farm to feed their families.

Guingané's play addresses the conflict between tradition and modernity during a health crisis. His characters personify certain modes of behavior, certain personalities, and certain attitudes when faced with a choice between traditional and modern concepts. One of the characters, Joe, addressing the audience directly tells them that he wants to talk about the rights of children. He represents the voice of the author and sets the background for the audience to understand the motif of the play. Another character, Ladji, is a father who does not exactly meet his responsibility toward his children. He is so fanatically attached to his traditional way of doing things that he refuses to send his sick child to the hospital for treatment.

Hence, the question Guingané poses in this play is how one can educate Burkinabé society to understand that African society as a whole has a lot to benefit from both traditional medicine and modern medicine available in hospitals. In general, people do not like to abandon their old ways of curing ailments. Yet, African society cannot refuse to benefit from Western medicine, which cures some of the ailments that traditional medicine has not been able to cure. Guingané is not necessarily suggesting a superiority of one mode of healing over another. However, he dramatizes conflicting modes of thought in contemporary society.

The play thus dramatizes real problems faced by society. These problems are currently being addressed through some of the UNICEF programs in the country. UNICEF programs have sought to educate people on basic hygienic practices, especially in rural areas. Yet, one must respect the customs and traditions of the people if such programs are to have any positive impact on Burkinabé society. People often tend to regard modern solutions to contemporary problems with suspicion if they see them as a challenge to their perceived notions of the world. Other people, however, are more successful in balancing traditional beliefs with Western modes of thought. For example, in Guingané's play, Fati teaches Ladji's wife how to cure her sick child with simple hygienic practices and with the correct dose of medicine. The character Ladji, however, believes strongly that all midwives are witches because their activities are similar to those of traditional healers who are believed to possess supernatural powers. Thus, he applies a traditional mode of thought to a modern concept of medicine.

Yet, through the same character Ladji, the playwright also introduces another element of conflict concerning the traditional concepts of the role of women. Ladji lacks respect for one of his wives, Bintou, because they do not have a son. Ladji's friend Moussa seemingly becomes the playwright's mouthpiece when he admonishes Ladji to have respect for all his wives as well as for all his children. After all, they are a gift from God, according to Moussa: "Ladji, un croyant ne doit pas raisonner comme tu le fais. L'enfant, qu'il soit fille ou garçon est un don de Dieu" [Ladji, a believer must not reason the way you do. The child, whether a girl or a boy, is God's gift]. Ladji also tends to blame many things on another wife, the one with whom he has a son called Mahamoudou; even the bad character of Mahamoudou is supposedly her fault. In fact, however, it is Ladji himself who is responsible for Mahamoudou becoming a delinquent. It is he who refused to feed him and to send him to school. Mahamoudou himself publicly accuses the father of being an irresponsible parent when he is arrested by the police for drug trafficking and brought home for a search of his parents' home. In African society, it is the sign of a serious lack of moral responsibility for a father to be publicly told that he is not capable of taking care of his children.

Western society has brought about modern urban dwellings that are attractive to young people dreaming of acquiring Western goods and Western ways of life. Mahamoudou, once he is away from the family, succumbs to the temptations of city life and turns into a juvenile delinquent. As long as he lives in the city, he is unable to benefit from the social responsibility incumbent upon the family and the village to bring him up as a responsible citizen. Thus, he becomes a victim not only of his father's careless behavior but also of the attractions of modern life. He is torn between simple village life and its depravations, and the "glamour" of city life with its potential for adventure.

Gender and Generational Differences in the Conflict of Cultures

In his short story "La Mendiante," Lézin Didier also questions certain traditions that tend to penalize women by blaming them for what are in fact acts of nature. It is the story of a rich man, Ladji, who shows pity and generosity toward a beggar who turns out to be his biological mother. Before her death, Manégré, the adoptive mother of Ladji, tells him how she had been maltreated and spited by her co-wives because of her inability to bear children. She says: "J'étais la risée de tout le monde" [I was the laughing stock of everyone]. The story is not a critique of the value that is attached to having children, but of the notion that women should be blamed when they are unable to conceive.

In the same story, the author also critiques society's attitude toward twins. Because of certain religious beliefs, they are considered a curse on the family and the community and are to be disposed of. In Ménéga, according to the story, it was the custom not to raise twins. Rather, twins were to be buried alive in an anthill where they were left to die to ward off curses.

The message of this short story is an admonition to fight for the rights of women and children alike. Burkinabé society, and by extension African society, needs to re-examine those customs and practices, including religious beliefs, that encourage the unjust treatment of women and children. Clinging to outmoded traditions is in direct conflict with notions of modernity and development. However, it is not merely a question of a conflict between Western culture and traditional culture, it is also a question of a conflict of ideas between different generations.

Traditional religious and social practices toward women and children are also depicted by other Burkinabé writers, especially short story writers. Clémentine Ilboudo's short story titled "Pougyounga" also deals with the gender issue and is one of the recent fictional modes through which Burkinabé writers deal with such issues in the context of the conflict between tradition and modernity. In Ilboudo's story, Tipoko has become the prototype of the submissive wife in traditional society. The omniscient narrator reveals to the reader the inner voice of Pougyounga, Tipoko's daughter, who plans to "liberate" herself from what she considers to be subjugation sanctioned by the traditions and customs of her people. She forges a relationship with Raïsa, a city girl who is determined to help her free herself from the oppressive customs of her family and from traditions they consider outmoded. Pougyounga's parents want her to marry an old man whom she does not even know. As a potential agent for Pougyounga's liberation from oppressive traditions and from a family that fails to understand that traditions must evolve with time, Raïsa advises Pougyounga to revolt against the family by moving away to the city. This act symbolizes a revolt against society as a whole with its norms and customs. As Raïsa says emphatically to Pougyounga: "Une fille comme toi mérite mieux qu'un vieux ramolli" (69) [a girl such as you deserves better than an old soft-headed fool].

Characters in a short story cannot evolve as much as in a novel simply because of the time limitations within the story and the implicit brevity of this genre. Nonetheless, as a character, Pougyounga evolves because of her relationship with Raïsa. The latter symbolizes the younger generation as it questions and revolts against certain traditions. The gift of a necklace from Pougyounga to Raïsa and the fact that Raïsa remodels it is a symbol of how she thinks society should be. She restructures the necklace so that it can be worn in many different ways, yet the beauty of each of its parts is seen equally. In other words, the necklace symbolizes the quest for equality for all in Burkinabé society, and more generally, in African society. The question of equality is raised in the context of intergenerational conflicts. For example, members of the older generation, represented by Pougyounga's parents do not embrace a society that would allow Pougyounga and Raïsa to revolt against or even to question their elders. Conversely, parents want to hold on to traditions, such as the passive obedience of children.

The end of Ilbouldo's story, however, does not offer a definite solution, as one would expect from the short story genre. In fact, it could be interpreted as the author's deliberate intent to leave the end of her story open to possible interpretations. Suspense is created because the reader does not know whether or not Raïsa and Pougyounga succeed in their bid to revolt against the customs of their people. Their migration to the urban center is escapist because this reaction will not necessarily change the mentality of the older generation. On the contrary, it might reinforce their belief that modernity represented by the urban area is only a counter-discourse to long-cherished traditions. An escape to the city could be perceived as defeatist because in this environment, the closely-knit family and clan do not have as much control over the individual's decisions and lifestyle. Cities are associated with Western culture as well as with the loss of social and moral values. Ilbouldo's story does not develop beyond the revolt against traditions in the village and an escape to the city in the hope of living a better life. It thus leaves the reader wondering if the message in the story could not have been developed further.

Henri Lamko Koulsy's short story "Un cadavre sur l'Epaule" also deals with gender issues and with the theme of escape to the city. In Koulsy's story, however, the urban area does not represent liberation. Rather, it becomes a symbol of the vicious cycle of oppression and exploitation of women. Furthermore, it symbolizes in a significant way the notion of a conflict between tradition and Western culture, and in a larger sense, between cultures. Koulsy's story addresses women's and children's rights. At the death of the narrator's father, the extended family takes his property, while ignoring completely his widow and children: "La tradition toute puissante exige bien que l'on se partage les richesses du défunt, ses enfants et même ses femmes" (92). [The all-powerful tradition demands that the wealth, the children, and even the wives of the deceased be shared]. The narrator's mother, refusing to live with the man who has "inherited" her as his fifth wife, then commits suicide:

> Elle s'était enfoncée une flêche empoisonnée dans le cœur. Pour les uns, c'était une bêtise, une marque de lâcheté; pour les autres, un acte de bravouac, un martyre. Pour elle, ce devait être une délivrance. Mes sœurs et moi, quant à nous, nous avions senti le ciel nous tomber sur la tête. (93)

> [She pierced a poisonous arrow through her heart. For some people, it was a foolish act, a sign of cowardice. For others, it was an act of bravery, of martyrdom. For her it must have been a deliverance. As for my sisters and me, we had felt the sky falling on our heads].

The narrator appeals to the reader's sensibility by suggesting that her mother's suicide was an act of deliverance from a family that had total disregard for the rights of a widow and her children. The fact that members of the community reacted differently to the widow's suicide depending on their ages also suggests a conflict of generations.

The narrator herself seems to be destined for a tragic life, too. The city is not a liberating space for her, but rather a place where the exploitation of women is played out. The narrator meets Cyril and falls in love with him. He takes her home but later abandons her when she announces to him that she is expecting his child. Moreover, her aunt's husband scolds her because she has taken two tablets and given medication to her sick child. Due to a lack of further medical care, the child dies. For the narrator, after all of her traumatic experiences, men have no heart. Koulsy's short story thus illustrates not only gender conflicts but also a conflict of generations and of cultures. Tension is created by different worldviews at play in the relationship between the characters.

Yet, not all the characters in these short stories take an escapist approach to the conflict of cultures. For example, in Ignace Hien's "Chic Choc," Bèro is courting Jeanne, but the latter decides she will marry another man, Jean, in order to please Jean's family. However, Jeanne does not ultimately succumb to family pressure. At the time of marriage, Jeanne refuses to marry the groom; thus she revolts against family members who think their interests supersede her own. These conflicts are shown to arise out of a perversion of traditions and customs in the short story.

The Questioning of Religious Beliefs

Sometimes, the conflict is a clash between religion and modern medicine. As Mamadou Barro suggests in his short story "Un Chapelet de Misères," saying one's prayers by reciting the beads is not sufficient to cure one's illnesses. The author does not criticize Islam per se, but rather any tendency to reject modern medicine with the belief that prayers alone can cure illnesses. There is a subtle critique of religious leaders who attempt to convince people that their miracles can cure diseases. This short story evokes a fundamental conflict of cultures that often arises between Islam and certain Western modes of solving physical and psychological problems. The same conflict is evoked in terms of a clash between traditional healing methods and modern Western medicine.

Salif Ousséni Napon evokes the problem of the role of religion in the conflict between traditionalism and modernity in his story titled, "La Vieille Kapouri." In a small village called Tchajassou, many people die suddenly without falling ill. The village community is eager to find an explanation for this mystery. An old lady, Kapouri, is accused of being a sorcerer and of being responsible for all the deaths among the young people. Since she has lost her husband and her children, there is nobody in the village to defend her against malicious accusations. Thus she becomes the target of all suspicions. The village magician, Avloui, consults the spirits of the dead and declares that Kapouri is the culprit, and Kapouri is then ostracized. But a little girl, Kouboutié, develops a strong love for this old lady. Her older sister, Kora, is inspired by this manifestation of love. Indeed, she calls a meeting of the Council of Elders to talk to them about the unjust way in which the community is treating the old lady. The Elders, however, ignore Kora's plea, and without giving Kapouri the chance to defend herself, they kill her. Still, after the murder, people continue to die mysteriously. The end of this story does not leave the reader indifferent. Kapouri is unjustly treated because there is no adult to defend her. The behavior of the community is based on a religious belief that seems to justify exterminating someone because she is suspected of using mysterious powers to kill people in the community.

In Guingané's play, *Papa Oublie-moi*, the playwright adds another dimension to the conflict between tradition and modernity. The playwright attempts to show that people who claim to safeguard tradition are not necessarily following tradition themselves. Sometimes, individuals pervert traditions in order to justify their own lifestyles. Religion can also be distorted for such ends. In the play, Ladji and his friend Moussa exploit children and "sell" them to the Islamic leader they call "Maître." They deprive the children of formal education, thus destroying their chances of getting good jobs in the modern economy where diplomas are essential to obtain any meaningful employment. Speaking bad French (thus creating a lot of humor), Sarzan gives them a moral lesson about the need to vaccinate their children and then takes the children to the hospital himself. The play poses the crucial question of how rural people in particular can reconcile their notions of medical treatment with the modern necessity for health care such as the vaccination of children against certain tropical diseases.

Conclusion

The works discussed here illustrate in fictional form the clash of cultures and values that plays itself out in contemporary Burkinabé society. Social structures change because people pursue divergent interests. In addition, there are other external as well as internal pressures toward change, and the more these changes come about, the greater the resistance of those who want to cling to traditions. The experience of Burkina Faso reinforces Cabral's observation that the elite in society might yearn for Western modes of life while using slogans about cultural authenticity and the need to safeguard traditional values. The social and political transformation that Burkinabé society has undergone since its contact with French culture demonstrates that the experience with civilian and military rule is part of society's struggle to come to terms with its past and with contemporary changes and transformations. These experiences are not limited to members of society who have been trained in French established schools, but pervade every class of the society.

A conflict of cultures is not unique to Burkina Faso. It is a common phenomenon in all African countries. One cannot discuss the issue of tradition and modernity in contemporary African society without analyzing the dynamics of its contact with Western culture. Cultures are ever changing, and African culture would have evolved even without contact with the West. Nonetheless, the clash of cultures in Burkina Faso has resulted from the imposition of Western culture on the minds of young Africans. This legacy has been sustained through Western systems of education, governance, and economic life. This conflict of cultures has made it crucial for Burkinabé people to continuously question their modes of contact with the West in the contemporary world, for such contact tends to be to the detriment of maintaining their own cultural identity.

Modernization is often advocated as a means of improving the lives of the Burkinabé people in particular and Africans in general, because it is argued that such modernization frees people from economic dependency. But close observation of the experience of Burkina Faso and other African countries shows how so-called modernization often creates a paradox. It destroys traditional modes of life while failing to replace them with modern modes that are sustainable and viable for the cultural and economic development of the people. Modernization is distrusted as a process that engenders vast disparities of wealth and subverts the cherished values of traditional societies (Bjornson 10). The authors and political observers mentioned in this study are not here advocating a society that sticks to outmoded values, but rather one whose conscience has been raised regarding the dangers of an uncritical assimilation of foreign cultures. A people who loses its culture in this kind of process loses its identity. As Derrida has theorized, we must master how to speak the other's language without renouncing our own (Derrida 333).

This is the challenge for Burkina Faso and other African nations as they strive to maintain their cultural authenticity in the face of changes and in the face of problems common to other African countries in the wake of the French colonialist era. Cultural authenticity in Burkina Faso will only be meaningful when the people in that multicultural society can speak the language of the West without renouncing their own.

NOTES

1. The Burkinabé historians Joseph Ki-Zerbo and Nazi Boni among others have written about the French colonial enterprise in what was then Upper Volta. Nazi Boni in particular writes about how the indigenous people resisted the French military invasion in the region. See Joseph Ki-Zerbo, *Histoire de l'Afrique Noire: D'hier à demain* (Paris: Hatier, 1972). Nazi Boni, *Histoire synthétique de l'Afrique résistante: Les réactions des peuples africains face aux influences extérieures* (Paris: Présence Africaine, 1971). Also see Nazi Boni's historical novel, *Crépuscule des temps anciens* (Paris: Présence Africaine, 1962).

2. All translations are my own.

REFERENCES

Barro, Mamadou. "Un chapelet de misères." *La Mendiante et Neuf autres Nouvelles.* Ed. Didier Lézin. Ouagadougou: Editions la Muse, 1993. 178–200.

Betts, Raymond. *Assimilation and Association in French Colonial Theory: 1890–1914.* New York: Columbia University Press, 1961.

Bjornson, Richard. *The African Quest for Freedom and Identity: Cameroonian Writing and the National Experience.* Bloomington: Indiana University Press, 1991.

Boni, Nazi. *Crépuscule des temps anciens.* Paris: Présence Africaine, 1962. *Histoire synthétique de l'Afrique résistante: Les réactions des peuples africains face aux influences extérieures.* Paris: Présence Africaine, 1971.

Cabral, Amilcar. "National Liberation and Culture." *Colonial Discourse and Post-Colonial Theory: A Reader.* Eds. Patrick Williams and Laura Chrisman. New York: Columbia University Press, 1994. 53–65.

Crowder, Michael. *Senegal: A Study in French Assimilation Policy.* London: Oxford University Press, 1962.

Derrida, Jacques. "Racism's Last Word." *"Race," Writing, and Difference.* Ed. Henry Louis Gates, Jr. Chicago: University of Chicago Press, 1986. 329–38.

Didier, Lézin. "La Mendiante." *La Mendiante et Neuf autres Nouvelles.* Ed. Didier Lézin. Ouagadougou: Editions la Muse, 1993. 6–26.

Gadjigo, Samba. *Ecole Blanche: Afrique Noire.* Paris: L'Harmattan, 1990.

Guingané, Jean-Pierre. *Papa, Oublie-Moi.* Ouagadougou: UNICEF: Théâtre de la Fraternité, 1990.

Herskovits, Melville. *Cultural Relativism: Perspectives in Cultural Pluralism.* New York: Random House, 1972.

Hien, Ignace A. "Chic Choc." *La Mendiante et Neufs autres Nouvelles.* Ed. Didier Lézin. Ouagadougou: Editions la Muse, 1993. 118–38.

Ilboudo Clémentine. "Pougyounga." *La Mendiante et Neuf autres Nouvelles.* Ed Didier Lézin. Ouagadougou: Editions la Muse, 1993. 49–80.

Ki-Zerbo, Joseph. *Histoire de l'Afrique Noire: D'hier à demain.* Paris: Hatier, 1972.

Koulsy, Henri Lamko. "Un Cadavre sur l'Epaule." *La Mendiante et Neuf autres Nouvelles.* Ed. Didier Lézin. Ouagadougou: Editions la Muse, 1993. 82–95.

Napon, Salif Ousséni. "La Vieille Kapouri." *La Mendiante et Neuf autres Nouvelles.* Ed. Didier Lézin. Ouagadougou: Editions la Muse, 1993. 28–47.

DISCUSSION QUESTIONS

1. How did France perceive its colonial mission in Africa and how did that determine its cultural policies in Africa?

2. Historically, how was the contact between African culture and Western culture created in Burkina Faso?

3. What was the mode of formal education introduced by the French in colonial Upper Volta?

4. What does Amilcar Cabral's theory of European cultural imperialism suggest about the reaction of Africans to colonialism in Africa?

5. How does the conflict of generations in Africa reflect the conflict between tradition and modernity?

6. How is gender an issue in the clash of cultures as suggested by the authors whose works are analyzed in this article?

❖ CHAPTER THREE

The Special Status of Senegal and the Emergence of Women Writers

Susan Stringer

A Brief History of Senegal

Senegal occupied a privileged political and cultural position in the French colonial system. From the fifteenth century on, various European powers fought for control of the coastal trading posts, largely because of their geographical importance in the slave trade. During the nineteenth century, however, the French conquered the interior and became undisputed masters of the region. As early as 1821 the first government was appointed with the mission of developing the region as a center of French civilization and the first schools were opened the following year.

From 1872 to 1887 the communes of Gorée, Saint-Louis, Rufisque, and Dakar were established. They were unique in that they offered their residents the rights to French citizenship and therefore to direct representation in the National Assembly in Paris. Men from these four communes could participate fully in the political process, holding elected office if they satisfied certain educational requirements.[1] In addition, they escaped the servitude imposed on their countrymen in the interior who were classified as "subjects" not citizens.

In 1887, the Ecole Normale William Ponty, the teachers' college that trained many future African leaders, was founded on the island of Gorée. In 1904, Dakar replaced Saint-Louis as the capital of French West Africa, a confederation of eight territories formed within the French colonial system in 1895.[2] Each territory had a large measure of autonomy with its own governor and territorial assembly. All, however, were subject to the governor-general in Dakar. The Institut Français d'Afrique Noire (I.F.A.N) was established in Dakar in 1938, and in 1959 the University of Dakar was inaugurated to serve the whole of French West Africa. In this way, Senegal became the administrative and educational center of French-speaking Black Africa.

The Unity of Senegal

Since precolonial times Senegal has had more natural unity based on religious

and ethnic considerations than other parts of Africa. More than ninety percent of Senegalese are Moslems (Gellar 88). Although only about one-third
of the population is ethnically Wolof, the Wolof language is understood by
most people (Blair 7). In fact, it is the "national" language of the country and
the most important second language for non-Wolofs. French, however, is the
"official" language of Senegal. In contrast, French is by necessity the *lingua
franca* in more linguistically and ethnically varied countries previously under
French rule. Michael Crowder sums up the unique circumstances of Senegal in
sub-Saharan Africa: "Nearly three-quarters of the population have closer historical and ethnic connections than exist in any other area of West Africa save
Hausaland in Northern Nigeria" (77). The relatively high rate of urbanization
at independence also contributed to the partial elimination of tribal differences
(Fougeyrollas 33).

The Intellectual Role of Senegal

The French administrative and educational concentration on Senegal led to
the emergence from Senegal of the first Black African intellectuals. Arguably
the most famous Senegalese of the twentieth century, the poet and statesman
Léopold Senghor (born in 1906) was the first Black African to be elected to the
Académie Française in 1983. He helped initiate the Negritude movement in the
thirties to give Blacks a voice through literature. Another Senegalese, Alioune
Diop, founded the publishing house and accompanying journal *Présence Africaine* in 1947. Both have played an important role in the development of African
literature and African studies. Since 1971 an equally significant contribution has
been made by another publishing company, Les Nouvelles Editions Africaines.
It originally operated only from Dakar, but now has branches in Abidjan (Ivory
Coast) and Lomé (Togo).

The Beginnings of African Literature in French

Poetry

Despite its association with Senghor and therefore Senegal, the Negritude
movement was international in aims and scope. Its primary genre was poetry,
an excellent medium through which to voice revolt. In fact, Africans and Blacks
in other parts of the francophone world initially expressed their protests against
colonialism and political and social injustice through poetry. The crowning
point of the Negritude crusade was the publication in 1948 of Senghor's now
famous *Anthologie de la nouvelle poésie nègre et malgache de langue française*
with the equally famous preface by Jean-Paul Sartre.

The Novel

By the 1950s it was clear that colonialism was a dying force, and in the period of transition preceding independence the novel became more important than poetry as a reflection of the new reality. The novel is suited to the presentation and analysis of social change in a way that poetry is not. Although a number of novels appeared before the fifties, including *Karim* by the Senegalese Ousmane Socé (1935), the publication of *L'Enfant noir* by the Guinean Camara Laye in 1953 is usually regarded as the real beginning of the West African francophone novel as an influential means of literary expression. Laye was closely followed by the Cameroonians Mongo Beti and Ferdinand Oyono and by a group of celebrated Senegalese novelists, including Abdoulaye Sadji, Cheikh Hamidou Kane, and Sembène Ousmane. All of these writers exposed in their own way the problems of colonialism and cultural conflict, of racial oppression and prejudice, and of the loss of traditional values.

The Role of Senegal

Senegal has continued to produce outstanding writers, playing an exceptional role in the development of African literature. In the preface to her *Senegalese Literature: A Critical History* (1984), Dorothy Blair says that she used to argue against the existence of national literatures in Africa, but now believes that Senegal is an exception. As Laurence Porter points out in his 1993 article: "A small population has produced an astonishing amount of first-rate literature" (887).

Women's Writing

The first francophone Black African woman to publish a collection of poems was the Senegalese Annette M'Baye, whose *Poèmes africains* appeared in 1965. However, there were no women among the first wave of African novelists. In fact, novels by African women did not appear until well into the sixties and then only in English-speaking countries. French-speaking women began to publish a decade later and remained largely unknown or ignored until the eighties. Some commentators attribute the time-gap between the appearance of anglophone and francophone women writers to the differences between the British and the French colonial school systems. Other observers blame Islam, but no unequivocal, undeniable causes can be established.

The Traditional Status of Women

The reasons for the delay in the emergence of women writers anywhere in Black

Africa are in dispute. Yet, despite the existence of often virulent disagreement both inside and outside the continent about the status of African women and about the role of religion, colonialism, and westernization in the retardation or advancement of that status, evidence appears to support a strong traditional bias toward male supremacy in most African societies. Research also suggests (see Hafkin and Bay; Van Allen) that colonialism reduced female rights because the colonial powers dealt only with men, even in the domain of agriculture, normally controlled by women.

Women and Formal Education

Whatever the traditional situation of women, in the French colonial school system they formed a small percentage of what was already a tiny elite. Very few children, male or female, went to colonial schools for any length of time. Crowder says that in 1938 there were 18,000 boys but only 1,500 girls attending school in Senegal (27). According to Omar Ka, in 1964-65 only eleven percent of Senegalese males and one percent of females said they could read and write French (278). These data indicate that the great majority of Senegalese men and an even greater majority of women were illiterate in the Western sense of the term because West African languages were not traditionally written. Nor did the existence of Koranic schools lead to general literacy in Arabic. In fact, outsiders often blame Islam for the lack of formal education for women, although this assertion is hotly contested by some Senegalese themselves.

African Attitudes toward Female Education

What is clear is that the colonial school system was seen to interfere with traditional female upbringing, carried out by the mother and grandmother and designed to produce a competent and submissive wife and mother. In addition, women were viewed as the guardians of tradition. Therefore, it was considered necessary to protect them against the alienating influences of what was essentially a foreign system, even after independence. Nevertheless, lack of education and hence of fluency in French may be only partly responsible for the lack of women writers. In Africa women are expected to be inconspicuous or to remain silent in public, an attitude confirmed by two of Senegal's most celebrated female novelists. In her journal article, Mariama Bâ claims that African women are reluctant to put their thoughts into print because social criticism is an unacceptable female activity (6). Aminata Sow Fall makes the same point in a 1985 interview with Françoise Pfaff. She says that writing is a form of boldness, shunned by women because they have been taught to be discreet (136).

The First Senegalese Novels by Women

Nafissatou Diallo

When francophone women finally began to publish, Senegalese writers were among the first. All available bibliographies of women's writing from franco-phone Black Africa attest to the primary role of Senegal, the only Moslem state to produce a sizeable literary corpus (see Christine Guyonneau in particular). As is the case with male authors, novels are the primary mode of expression for women. Because they now number more than twenty, it is not possible to analyze each one separately here. Yet it is instructive to highlight the beginnings because of what they reveal about African literature in general and women's literature in particular.

The publication of Nafissatou Diallo's *De Tilène au Plateau* in 1975 is regarded as the birth of feminine literature from French-speaking Black Africa. In the preface to her autobiographical account of growing up in Dakar before independence, Diallo feels obliged to justify writing the book. Adopting an apologetic tone, she is at pains to present herself as an ordinary Senegalese woman with no particular talents. Even so, she says she wishes to record a disappearing world for the modern generation. Within the text itself she also emphasizes her desire to serve as the collective memory for her beloved family, presented as cultural models. Thus Diallo has chosen the autobiographical form because she sees herself as representative, not only of her family, but also of her community and her generation. (The work is subtitled "une enfance dakaroise" [a Dakar childhood]).

This collective function is common to most African literature, and there is a revealing parallel between Diallo's stated aims and those of her precursor in male writing, Camera Laye. In a paper entitled "The Soul of Africa in Guinea," presented when he was already a celebrity, Laye underlines his own representa-tive role as "l'enfant noir" [the Black child] of his first novel. Thus in speaking out for her own gender, Diallo treads the same path as Laye two decades before. She did for African women in 1975 what he had done for men in 1953.

Aminata Sow Fall and Mariama Bâ

Yet Diallo's autobiography passed almost unnoticed. So did the first novel of Aminata Sow Fall, now the *Grande Dame* of francophone Black African letters, who published *Le Revenant* in 1976. In fact, 1979 was a far more important seminal year for women's writing. In that year Sow Fall's second novel *La Grève des Bàttu* was shortlisted for the Prix Goncourt, and Mariama Bâ published *Une Si Longue Lettre*, both works appearing in English translation in 1981. Bâ received the Noma award for the best overseas novel in French in 1980, and

Sow Fall won the Grand Prix Littéraire de L'Afrique Noire in 1981.

Of the two novels, *Une Si Longue Lettre* caused a greater stir, and it has remained to this day the most famous francophone novel by a West African woman, perhaps because of its overt feminism. This first-person narration in the form of one long letter to a friend, very much akin to a diary, presents the thoughts of the protagonist, Ramatoulaye, as she goes through the forty-day mourning period for the husband who abandoned her for a young girl after many years of marriage. Although the work has autobiographical origins, the novelistic form gives Bâ full rein to explore the trials and tribulations of the narrator as she attempts to come to peace with herself and dispel the anger and bitterness incited by her husband's conduct. The combination of intimacy and representation is the key to the novel's enormous success. As Bâ points out in an interview with Barbara Harrell-Bond, not only Islamic Senegalese women, but all women can identify with Ramatoulaye.

Feminism in Women's Writing

Women's writing from Senegal does not always have an overt feminist purpose. In her second novel *Un Chant écarlate*, Bâ avoids such an approach by choosing a male protagonist; yet she ultimately tells basically the same story of male infidelity and treachery with the extra dimension of an interracial marriage.

Unlike Bâ, Sow Fall stresses in her many interviews that she is not a feminist novelist, nor has she written anything even vaguely autobiographical. All her protagonists are male, and all but one of her novels are written in the third person with multiple viewpoints. Yet there is in each of Sow Fall's works a strong female character who, because of her influence over the action, her relationship to the main theme, and her power over the main character could be defined as a hidden protagonist.

Sow Fall could therefore be defined as a different sort of feminist from Bâ. Although there are oppressed women in her books, she does not use her main female characters to protest against the injustices of the feminine condition but to reveal the potential of strong women to change society. Despite her claims about being more interested in general social issues than in gender, she shares with other Senegalese women writers a preoccupation with women, a manifest distinction between male and female writing.

Other women writers appeared after Diallo, Bâ, and Sow Fall. Some of them belong to the same generation, and some are younger. Yet there exists in all the female literature not just the common bond of a female perspective but also a remarkable communality of themes, if not always agreement. Senegalese women writers emphasize the personal relationships and the inner development of the individual woman, thus producing a variety of rounded characters rather than stereotypes. At the same time, these characters serve as models, both negative and positive.

Types of Female Characters in Women's Writing

Despite the avoidance of cardboard female stereotypes commonly found in writing by African men (especially in earlier years) some female types can be distinguished in women's writing. It should be emphasized, however, that many characters fit into more than one category.

The Mother

The mother is an important presence, but she is not mythologized or sanctified as in some female writing from Africa, although she may be a respected matriarch. Normally she is devoted to her children. Sometimes she is a victim. Another recurring figure is the grandmother or mother as friend or accomplice. There are also a few examples of the destructive mother or mother-in-law, the most striking illustration of which is in Aïcha Diouri's novelette, *La Mauvaise Passe,* where a young boy resorts to a street life of theft, alcoholism, and drugs because of his mother's abuse.

More prominently, however, the mother in the Senegalese novels has a contrastive function in relation to the younger generation, particularly to her daughter. She illustrates a conservative mentality with its acceptance of an imposed lifestyle, while the daughter represents the modern woman refusing to accept traditional limitations on her freedom of action. The result is conflict, even if the relationship is good. This contrasting viewpoint about the female condition in an essentially harmonious relationship appears in Bâ's *Une Si Longue Lettre,* in Sow Fall's *La Grève des Bàttu, L'Ex-père de la nation, Le Jujubier du patriarche* and in Ka's *La Voie du salut* and *En Votre Nom et au mien.*

More rarely, the bond between mother and child is profoundly disturbed by the difference in mentality, leading to a breakdown of the relationship. This is the case with Adji Arame and Ndeye in Ka's *Le Miroir de la vie* and Tante Ngoone and Faatim in Khadi Fall's *Mademba.* Diattou and her son Nalla in Sow Fall's *L'Appel des arènes* incarnate a reversal of the norm. He wishes to reestablish his links with tradition, while she totally rejects the past. These generational differences highlight the fact that cultural change or conflict is the mainspring of all the writing.

The Young Unmarried Woman

Cultural conflict may also exist as an internal struggle within the young woman herself, as in the case of Ken Bugul in her poignant and powerful autobiography, *Le Baobab fou*. Generally, however, the young woman does not incorporate conflict. She is either traditional (Nabou in Bâ's *Une Si Longue Lettre* and Ouleymatou in Bâ's *Un Chant écarlate*) or modern (Daba in *Une Si Longue Lettre*, Raabi and Sine in Sow Fall's *La Grève des Bàttu*, Nafi in Sow Fall's *L'Ex-Père de la nation*, Rabiatou in Ka's *La Voie du salut* and Faatim in Khadi Fall's *Mademba*).

In Bâ's writing the male protagonist of *Un Chant écarlate*, Ousmane, is the strongest example of cultural conflict within the individual. Furthermore, in her first novel the mature married woman, Ramatoulaye most embodies the dialectic between tradition and progress. It is a mistake, therefore, to be too categorical about character types. Because of the social transformations taking place in Senegal, almost all the characters experience cultural conflict to some degree.

The Wife

The woman as wife is most notable in the novels of Bâ and Ka because of their interest in the relationship between couples. Wives are also prominent in Khadi Fall's *Mademba* and in Mbacke's story "Youmané l'Africaine exilée." But in Diallo's works and in Ken Bugul's autobiography, all the protagonists, except Fary in the second half of *La Princesse de Tiali,* are young unmarried women. Even if some married women are influential in Diallo's writing, they remain secondary figures. In the novels of Sow Fall, the main female characters are all married, but their marital status is irrelevant in comparison to their personal attributes. Other married women in Sow Fall's work reveal how marital experience can vary widely from one woman to another.

The Professional

The stress on the inner resources of the woman, on her self-confidence and values, could explain why so little attention is paid to her professional activities. Although a high proportion of the main female characters are professionals and others are students, this aspect of their lives is mostly mentioned but not shown. Those authors who choose educated women as main characters (and Sow Fall is a notable exception, apart from Diattou in *L'Appel des arènes*) prefer to expose the ambiguities of social transition through human relationships outside the work context. This approach perhaps reflects a view that the private rather than the public role of women is more instrumental in eventual change.

The authors thus concentrate on the particular aspect of a woman's existence most interesting to them as social commentators. They are more preoccupied with the individual's personal evolution and particularly with the element of choice in her life, rather than with one exclusive role.

Themes in the Novel

Marriage

The primacy of both personal life and choice makes marriage with all its attendant themes central to the novels. The first issue is whether a woman can select her own husband or not. What is surprising in Diallo's autobiography is that, although she comes from a traditional family, she actually chooses freely three times, finally marrying her third love. In all Diallo's works, except *Awa la petite marchande* where the protagonist is too young, the heroine alone decides on her partner and subsequently has a happy and fulfilling marriage.

Polygamy

Because the Islamic religion allows a man to have four wives at the same time, polygamy is widespread in Senegal and is a common literary theme. In novels by writers other than Diallo there are also women who select their own partner for love and sometimes intellectual compatibility, but they later feel betrayed and humiliated when the man then takes a second, younger wife after many years of marriage (Bâ's *Une Si Longue Lettre,* Sow Fall's *La Grève des Bàttu*). In some cases the man takes a second wife within a couple of years. Ousmane in Bâ's *Un Chant écarlate* marries a Senegalese girl without telling his French wife, causing her to become insane and kill their child. In Ka's *La Voie du salut,* Rabiatou collapses and dies when she hears of her husband's secret marriage to a courtesan.

Polygamy plays a significant role in most Senegalese novels by women. It is never presented positively and rarely neutrally. Even where it is accepted as natural, as in the traditional context of Diallo's historical novel *Le Fort maudit,* it is the cause of rivalry, dissention, and bitterness.

Arranged Marriages

Arranged marriages are also criticized in the modern context, particularly if a young girl is married off to an older man with one or more wives. This is the subject of Ka's *En Votre Nom et au mien* where Awa is forced into a loveless polygamous marriage by her parents because her young fiancé does not have the money to pay the dowry. She finally revolts against serving others' needs and is reunited with her first choice, now a man of education and influence. In

Une Si Longue Lettre, Binetou is persuaded by her mother's tears and supplications to marry Modou, Ramatoulaye's husband, because he has money, but the marriage destroys her youthful joy. Modou also insists that she leave school despite her interest and success in her studies.

The Caste System

The subject of marriage is sometimes used to condemn the survival of the Wolof caste system, traditionally divided into freemen, artisans, and slaves. Ramatoulaye's friend and addressee Aïssatou in *Une Si Longue Lettre* is the daughter of a goldsmith while her husband belongs to the nobility. From the beginning, her mother-in-law sets out to destroy the marriage by bringing up a young family member to be the second wife. Unlike Ramatoulaye, Aïssatou prefers divorce to polygamy. Caste is also significant in Diallo's *La Princesse de Tiali*, Ka's *Le Miroir de la vie*, and Khadi Fall's *Mademba*.

Religion

Senegalese women writers thus opt for free choice in marriage, but they show that it is no guarantee of success as long as polygamy is an easy option in an Islamic society. Although all the novelists under discussion directly or indirectly promote Islam, they are critical of religious hypocrisy supporting male polygamous instincts. One scene in Bâ's *Une Si Longue Lettre* exemplifies this distinction. Ramatoulaye is profoundly religious, but when a delegation led by the local *imam* (religious official) arrives at the house to inform her that by the will of God Modou has taken a second wife, she feels betrayed in both her marriage and her beliefs. Modou has ignored the religious requirement that his first wife be told in advance. In addition, he later disobeys the Islamic commandment to treat both wives equally.

Marabouts/Holy Men

Religious superstition especially in relation to *marabouts* (Muslim holy men) is also denounced. This is a frequent motif in African literature. Some *marabouts* are nothing more than charlatans (as in Diallo's *La Princesse de Tiali*). Others may really be holy men, but their followers' obsessive attachment to their recommendations seems to have little to do with genuine piety. The plot of Sow Fall's *La Grève des Bàttu* revolves around the attempts of the main character Mour to follow the *marabout*'s instructions to distribute meat and goods to the city beggars in the streets in order to gain the vice-presidency of the country. The beggars' strike makes the "charity" impossible, and Mour fails to be promoted. It is left to the reader to judge the reason why.

Money

Another theme related to the subject of marriage is that of money. Marriage is often an investment, leading to the enrichment of a woman and her family. This is the case of Fary in Diallo's *La Princesse de Tiali*, of Binetou in Bâ's *Une Si Longue Lettre*, of Ouleymatou in Bâ's *Un Chant écarlate,* of Yama in Sow Fall's *Le Revenant*, and of Yandé in Sow Fall's *L'Ex-père de la Nation.*

The novels also denounce the ruinous extravagance at ceremonies marking the different stages of life. Baptisms, marriages, and funerals are transformed into financial competitions between families to win prestige. The parasitism of the new African elite and generalized corruption, particularly in hospitals, are also condemned.

Money is shown to be the greatest source of power in modern Senegal. Sow Fall's *Le Revenant* was written precisely because the author was so shocked at the materialism she saw on returning home after seven years in France. Yet Diallo's *La Princesse de Tiali*, set in precolonial times, reveals that greed has always existed, even if money has not.

Education

The other aspect of a woman's life related to choice and personal development is education. Unlike marriage, toward which women writers have similar attitudes, education inspires either differing opinions or ambivalence.

In *De Tilène au Plateau* and *Awa la petite marchande*, Diallo makes formal education an essential element in personal and social success. Bâ shares this attitude in *Une Si Longue Lettre*. Ramatoulaye is a teacher totally committed to education for girls. In *Un chant écarlate*, however, Ousmane's education is problematic because he finally sees it as a source of alienation from his African roots.

Sow Fall exposes an even more tragic example of acculturation in *L'Appel des arènes* where Diattou's education combined with a stay in France make her despise everything authentically African, leading to the disintegration of her personal and professional life. Yet in the same novel, the schoolteacher Monsieur Niang personifies the harmonious reconciliation of modern education and traditional values.

In Ka's *La Voie du salut*, Rabiatou actually comes to appreciate Africa while completing her studies in France. Yet her brilliant intellectual achievements and social prominence as a magistrate, which first attract her husband's admiration, do not prevent him from abandoning her for a loose, uneducated woman.

The most virulent condemnation of formal schooling is to be found in Ken Bugul's *Le Baobab fou*. One of the *leit-motifs* of this heart-rending personal account is the lamentation about "the French school" as the primary cause of her traumatic alienation from family, village, and African traditions.

Thus the first novels saw education as the path to freedom and enlightenment for women. Very soon, however, women writers realized that formal education has its negative aspects, too. Even when not directly harmful, it is not a panacea for personal problems.

Cultural Conflict

The ambivalent attitude of Senegalese women writers to formal schooling reveals once again the supreme importance of cultural conflict as the mainspring of African writing. Even in the postcolonial era, education can be equated with westernization and acculturation. The basic problem for Senegalese society, as for the rest of the continent, is how to keep what is positive in tradition while participating in modern global life.

A significant Senegalese diaspora exists. In fact, parts of Diallo's *Awa la petite marchande*, Bâ's *Le Chant écarlate*, Ka's *La Voie du salut*, Mbacke's *Le Froid et le piment*, and the two novels of Bugul are set in France (or Belgium in the case of *Le Baobab fou*). Even those who never leave the country cannot divorce themselves from outside influences, especially as urbanization is a continuing process. Many Senegalese no longer have contact with a village, long portrayed in novels by men and women as the home of tradition. Frequent and prolonged drought has led to greater migration and impoverishment, and the latest novels reveal that Dakar has the same problems as other world cities: street children, gangs, alcoholism, and drugs.

The interdependence of rural societies, in which sharing was not just a religious duty but the foundation of existence, tends to disappear in an urban environment. Yet Sow Fall's latest novel *Le Jujubier du patriarche* claims that without the reestablishment of traditional African values with respect to the primacy of the community over the individual, there is no hope for the future.

The Role of Women Writers

Although Senegalese women are writing because they have something to say to everyone about contemporary Senegalese society and about their identity as Black Africans in a world threatened by Western economic and cultural domination, they are sending a special message to and about women. In their aspiration to reconcile positive traditional values and female emancipation, women suffer a double conflict, nonexistent for men. For the latter, it is simply a question of an opposition between tradition and modernity. Yet tradition sometimes conflicts directly with female emancipation, because it has often been oppressive to women, especially in marriage where they have been regarded as property. Senegalese women writers do not resolve this conflict. They show that each man and woman must reflect on the identity crisis and search for an appropriate solution. Yet they reveal that a profound change in the relationship between men and women is central to any process of modernization.

Despite the fact that female writing supports a form of individualism generally considered impossible in traditional society, the novelists plainly advocate an African individualism, firmly rooted in cultural identity. Whereas Western feminism has tried to create a feminist set of values, Senegalese women writers are trying to reconcile traditional moral norms with freedom of choice and see themselves as less antagonistic toward men than Western feminists. The central importance of motherhood and the firm belief in gender roles lead African women to look for a new form of partnership with men without sacrificing motherhood and marriage. These concerns are clearly reflected in the novels by Senegalese women.

NOTES

1. The first Black African elected to the National Assembly was Blaise Diagne in 1914.
2. These were Senegal, Guinea, Ivory Coast, French Sudan (now Mali), Dahomey (now Benin), Upper Volta (now Burkina Faso), Mauritania, and Niger.

REFERENCES

Bâ, Mariama. "La Fonction politique des littératures africaines écrites." *Ecriture française dans le monde* 5.1 (1981): 3–7.

———. *Un Chant écarlate*. Dakar: Les Nouvelles Editions Africaines, 1981.

———. *Une Si Longue Lettre*. Dakar: Les Nouvelles Editions Africaines, 1979.

Blair, Dorothy S. *Senegalese Literature: A Critical History*. Boston: Twayne, 1984.

Bugul, Ken. *Le Baobab fou*. Dakar: Les Nouvelles Editions Africaines, 1982.

Crowder, Michael. *Senegal. A Study in French Assimilation Policy*. London: Oxford University Press, 1962.

Diallo, Nafissatou. *Awa la petite marchande*. Dakar: Les Nouvelles Editions Africaines, 1981.

———. *De Tilène au Plateau*. Dakar: Les Nouvelles Editions Africaines, 1975.

———. *Le Fort maudit*. Paris: Hatier, 1980.

———. *La Princesse de Tiali*. Dakar: Les Nouvelles Editions Africaines, 1987.

Diouri, Aïcha. *La Mauvaise Passe*. Dakar: Khoudia, 1990.

Fall, Khadi. *Mademba*. Paris: L'Harmattan, 1989.

Fougeyrollas, Pierre. *Modernisation des hommes*. Paris: Flammarion, 1967.

Gellar, Sheldon. *Senegal: An African Nation between Islam and the West*. Boulder, Colorado: Westview Press, 1982.

Guyonneau, Christine H. "Francophone Women Writers from Sub-Saharan Africa: A Preliminary Bibliography." *Callaloo* 8.2 (1985): 453–83.

Hafkin, Nancy J., and Edna G. Bay, eds. *Women in Africa*. Stanford: Stanford University Press, 1976.

Harrell-Bond, Barbara. "Interview avec Mariama Bâ le 9 juillet 1979." *African Book Publishing Record* 6 (1980): 209–14.

Ka, Aminata Maïga. *La Voie du salut suivi de Le Miroir de la Vie*. Paris: Présence Africaine, 1985.

———. *En Votre Nom et au mien*. Abidjan: Les Nouvelles Editions Africaines, 1989.

Ka, Omar. "Une Nouvelle Place pour le français au Sénégal." *The French Review* 67.2 (December 1993): 276–90.

Laye, Camara. "The Soul of Africa in Guinea." *African Literature and the Universities*. Ed. Gerald Moore. Ibadan: Ibadan University Press, 1965: 64–73.

Mbacke, Mame Seck. *Le Froid et le piment*. Dakar: Les Nouvelles Editions Africaines, 1983.

Pfaff, Françoise. "Aminata Sow Fall: L'Ecriture au féminin." *Notre Librairie* 81 (1985): 135–38.

Porter, Laurence M. "Senegalese Literature Today." *The French Review* 66.6 (May, 1993): 887–99.

Sow Fall, Aminata. *L'Appel des arènes*. Dakar: Les Nouvelles Editions Africaines, 1982.

———. *L'Ex-père de la nation*. Paris: L'Harmattan, 1987.

———. *La Grève des Bàttu*. Dakar: Les Nouvelles Editions Africaines, 1979.

———. *Le Jujubier du patriarche*. Dakar: Khoudia, 1993.

———. *Le Revenant*. Dakar: Les Nouvelles Editions Africaines, 1976.

Van Allen, Judith. "Women in Africa. Modernization Means More Dependancy." *The Center Magazine* 7.3 (1974): 60–67.

SENEGALESE NOVELS BY WOMEN

Bâ, Mariama. *Un Chant écarlate*. Dakar: Les Nouvelles Editions Africaines, 1981.

———. *Scarlet Song*. Translated by Dorothy S. Blair. Harlow, Essex: Longman, 1985.

———. *Une Si Longue Lettre*. Dakar: Les Nouvelles Editions Africaines, 1979.

———. *So Long a Letter*. Translated by Modupé Bodé-Thomas. London: Heinemann, 1981.

Bugul, Ken. *Cendres et Braises*. Paris: L'Harmattan, 1994.

———. *Le Baobab fou*. Dakar: Les Nouvelles Editions Africaines, 1982.

———. *The Abandoned Baobab*. Translated by Marjolijn de Jager. Brooklyn, New York: Lawrence Hill Books, 1991.

Diallo, Nafissatou. *Awa la petite marchande*. Dakar: Les Nouvelles Editions Africaines, 1981.

———. *De Tilène au Plateau*. Dakar: Les Nouvelles Editions Africaines, 1975.

———. *A Dakar Childhood*. Translated by Dorothy S. Blair. Harlow, Essex: Longman, 1982.

———. *Le Fort maudit*. Paris: Hatier, 1980.

———. *La Princesse de Tiali*. Dakar: Les Nouvelles Editions Africaines, 1987.

———. *Fary, Princess of Tiali*. Translated by Anne Woollcombe. Washington, D. C.: Three Continents Press, 1987.

Diouri, Aïcha. *La Mauvaise Passe*. Dakar: Khoudia, 1990.

Fall, Khadi. *Mademba*. Paris: L'Harmattan, 1989.

Ka, Aminata Maïga. *La Voie du salut suivi de Le Miroir de la Vie*. Paris: Présence Africaine, 1985.

———. *En Votre Nom et au mien*. Abidjan: Les Nouvelles Editions Africaines, 1989.

Mbacke, Mame Seck. *Le Froid et le piment*. Dakar: Les Nouvelles Editions Africaines, 1983.

Ndiaye, Adja Ndeye. *Collier de cheville*. Dakar: Les Nouvelles Editions Africaines, 1983.

DISCUSSION QUESTIONS

1. How is Senegal different from other former French colonies in West Africa?

2. Why did the novel become more important than poetry?

3. Why did women start publishing later than men? Do you see any parallels with the situation here and in other countries?

4. To what extent can novels by Senegalese women be considered feminist? In your opinion, what is feminist writing?

5. What types of women are portrayed? Do these types exist in literature from other parts of the world?

6. Which themes seem particular to Africa and which seem universal?

7. How is the situation of women different from that of men with regard to cultural conflict?

8. Does literature enable us to understand foreign cultures?

9. In your opinion, for whom are these women are writing?

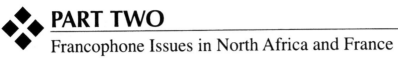

PART TWO

Francophone Issues in North Africa and France

CHAPTER FOUR

North Africans in France:
A Crisis in Cultural Identity—Tahar Ben Jelloun's
Les Raisins de la galère

Sylvie Charron and Sue Huseman

Introduction

In recent years, a number of books, feature articles, documentaries, and films such as Mathieu Kassovitz's *Hate* (1995) or Mahmoud Zemmouri's *100% Arabica* (1997), have brought to light the situation of North African immigrants in France and the barely improved condition of their families after two generations.[1] Tahar Ben Jelloun's novel *Les Raisins de la galère* is a particularly eloquent example of these efforts to focus attention on the plight of the *Maghrébins* in France, and in particular on the *Beurs* (second generation immigrants) who are French citizens but find themselves caught between two cultures, alienated from both.[2] With some striking exceptions, the *Beurs* rarely feel completely integrated into French society, and yet they have neither the ability nor the desire to return to an ancestral home that is now more foreign to them in language and culture than France itself.

Les Raisins de la galère is a novel, narrated in the first person from the point of view of a young Algerian girl living with her family in the suburbs of Paris. The narrator, Nadia, is intelligent, beautiful, and full of grand dreams; she is a good student and model adolescent. When the traditional Algerian house that her father has built in the center of town is razed by local administrators motivated by jealousy, greed, and covert racism, her rage at this injustice drives her to political action. Her activism puts her in touch with her community and reveals to her the complex web of economic, social, and political tensions surrounding her. In addition, she must deal with family tensions that result from clashing cultural and gender roles. The novel addresses the issues of racism and postcolonial urban ethnic oppression in a powerful and poetic voice. Ben Jelloun advocates for the fundamental human rights of immigrants to France from the former French colonies, especially from the Maghreb,[3] and emphasizes the important contributions these new citizens can make to French society. The novel is equally significant from a literary perspective, in its mixture of poetic prose and powerful street language. It is also unique in that the author writes across gender lines, using a female narrator as he does in many of his novels.

He also writes across cultural boundaries, as a Moroccan male writer speaking through the voice of a young Algerian woman living in France.

According to Tahar Ben Jelloun, the impetus to write *Les Raisins de la galère* came from Jean Orsena, the editor of the *Libres* collection at the Fayard publishing house. Orsena suggested that Ben Jelloun write a *Maghrébin* success story, for example the story of a successful athlete, to counter the consistently negative images and stereotypes of Arab immigrants reflected in the media such as the riots in the *cités*, genital mutilation, or the wearing of veils in public schools.[4]

Ben Jelloun considered writing about a particular member of the European parliament who was a woman of Algerian descent. However, since he did not know her personally, he decided to interview a local *Beur* politician who was running for municipal office in Sartrouville, a communist town near Paris. His novel is based in part on the information gathered from this brief interview, but it draws as well on the author's own perceptions and experience, and on his enormous narrative talent and imagination. Indeed, when the original inter-viewee read the novel, she was amazed by the accuracy with which it portrayed details of her experience she had not shared with the author.[5]

More about the Author and His Work

Tahar Ben Jelloun was born and raised in Morocco. He is now one of the most respected francophone writers currently living in France. He was born in 1944 and has written more than a dozen novels.[6] He received the prestigious Prix Goncourt in 1987 for *La Nuit sacrée* (1987), a sequel to *L'Enfant de sable* (1985). These two novels recount the many struggles associated with gender identity in the Muslim world. *La Nuit sacrée* sold about two million copies and was translated into more than forty languages. Ben Jelloun's other novels include *Harrouda* (1976), *Moha le fou, Moha le sage* (1979), *La Prière de l'absent* (1981), *L'Ecrivain public* (1983), *L'Homme rompu* (1994), and *La Nuit de l'erreur* (1997). Three novels, *La Réclusion solitaire* (1976), *Les Yeux baissés* (1991), and *Les Raisins de la galère* (1996), focus on the difficult and often traumatic experiences of immigrants.[7] Ben Jelloun frequently appears on French television and writes for the press. He has also written for the stage (*La Fiancée de l'eau*, 1984) and is a celebrated poet. In 1995, *Poésie complète* and a collection of short stories, *Le Premier amour est aussi le dernier*, were published by Seuil.[8]

In his work, Tahar Ben Jelloun has taken a strong stand against racism. His recent book, *Le Racisme expliqué à ma fille* (*Racism Explained to My Daughter*),[9] struck a deep chord with the French public and was on France's best-seller list for weeks after it first appeared in January 1998. The book explains the psy-

chology of racism to children at a time when the racist politics of the National
Front and its leader Jean-Marie Le Pen are becoming ever more ubiquitous and
powerful in France.[10]

In the introduction, Ben Jelloun explains what provided the impetus for this
essay against racism: "It was in February 1997, when my daughter and I went
to protest the Debré Law on entry requirements and guest permits for foreign
visitors to France that the idea for this book came to me" (*Le Racisme* 5). Ben
Jelloun had already expressed his outrage at the blatant racism of the new law
in an article for *Le Monde* (18 April 1997) entitled *"Ma mère ne viendra pas
en France"* (*My Mother Won't Come to France*), where he pointed out why
closing the door to foreign ideas and diversity makes no sense: "The notion of
a global French-speaking community is incompatible with the current politics
of immigration. What would these racist fanatics do with the French language
which includes literally thousands of foreign words? To begin with, they'd have
to expunge four thousand words of Arab origin."

The pedagogical orientation of *Le Racisme expliqué à ma fille* grows out
of the same conviction that underlies the novel *Les Raisins de la galère* (*The
Grapes of Despair*),[11] that the struggle against racism begins with education.
Both works are designed to bring this issue into the open and educate people.
Les Raisins achieves this by telling a story and *Le Racisme* by exploring intellectual concepts and explaining them in simple terms that schoolchildren will
understand.

A Brief History of North African Immigration to France

Les Raisins de la galère is the story of a North African immigrant family in the
Paris suburbs. Inhabitants from the Maghreb began immigrating to France in
large numbers following World War II. In 1974, during the first oil crisis, and
the massive factory shutdowns and unemployment that resulted, an immigration
office was established in France to put a stop to large-scale immigration. Moreover, in 1977, a law was passed to actively encourage immigrants to return to
their countries of origin by offering them a small stipend to leave France. Few
Maghrébins took advantage of this offer. Indeed, those who had immigrated to
France before the Algerian War of Independence were already French citizens,
as was any child born in France. Finally, in 1993, the Veil/Mehaignerie law was
passed, requiring children born on French soil of foreign parents to petition in
order to become French citizens.[12]

The *Maghrébins* were originally hired to work in factories, in construction, or in other unskilled jobs, such as in agriculture, at a time when France's
need for unskilled labor was intense. On their part, North Africans took any
employment they could find in order to feed their families back home. French

recruiters sought out unskilled workers from remote areas in North Africa, so that they would be illiterate, ill-prepared to demand or defend their rights, and likely to accept substandard or even subhuman living and working conditions. Men were usually hired for a fixed period of three years with the expectation that they would then return home to Africa. They were required to come to France alone and usually lived in shantytowns or unsanitary barracks provided by the companies or in some cases by the government. They returned to their villages for a two-month period each summer, but during the rest of the year they shared these barracks with hundreds of other men. As members of the French colonies or protectorates, they were also called up to serve in any armed conflict France was involved in, beginning with World War I, where many *Maghrébins* lost their lives. By and large, these immigrants accepted their fate without complaint for fear of being deported.[13]

In 1974, when France closed its doors to new immigrants, it also created a new family reunification law (*législation du regroupement familial*). This leg-islation allowed immigrants already in France to remain there and to bring their families to join them. To resolve the acute housing problems that this influx of family members caused, these new families were housed in transitory housing projects, the so-called *cités de transit*, dotted with flimsy, ill-equipped one-story structures, crisscrossed with unpaved streets and surrounded by fences. These *cités* resembled internment camps more than neighborhoods. Immigrant fami-lies were expected to stay in the *cités* for up to two years, until better housing became available and until French social workers could ensure their smooth transition into French culture by offering them literacy classes, health care, and nutrition training. In reality, many *Maghrébins* remained in these dwellings for over twenty years. They lived like prisoners, in some cases unable to leave the *cités* after 11p.m., because of a curfew imposed by the gatekeepers.[14]

It is significant that Ben Jelloun's novel focuses on a particular Algerian family in the Paris suburbs, because Algeria stands out among the Maghreb na-tions for the unparalleled violence and human displacement that marks its history. The Algerian War of Independence (1954–1962) was particularly brutal. It tore the country apart, displacing millions of citizens, without managing to resolve the fundamental political, economic, religious, and cultural tensions resulting from the colonial period. Between five hundred thousand and a million and a half Algerians lost their lives during the war.

After the war, a hundred and fifty thousand *Harki* soldiers (Algerians who had fought against the FLN or *Front de Libération Nationale*) were murdered in retaliation for war crimes, a million Algerian workers migrated to France, and about a million *Pieds noirs* (French colonists who had lived in Algeria for generations) were forced to leave Algeria.[15] At the same time, the FLN assumed power in Algeria without an open electoral process.

In 1989, a new constitution established a multi-party system, but in 1991, when the *Front Islamique du Salut* (FIS), a fundamentalist religious group, seemed poised to win the national elections, the army took over, banning the FIS in order to retain power. Random killings and atrocities of every kind ensued, including the systematic harassment of women, the murder of intellectuals and journalists, school shutdowns, rapes, torture, the destruction of property, and recurrent bomb threats.[16] Since 1992, at least seventy-five thousand civilians have lost their lives by official count, with each day bringing more bloodshed and misery.[17] It is little wonder that French immigrants of Algerian descent choose to remain in France despite the difficulties they face both in adapting to the new culture and in being accepted in it.

The Crisis in Cultural Identity

The crisis in cultural identity that confronts the *Maghrébin* immigrants to France is a complex one, resulting from tensions between the old and the new culture, and the traditions, values, and beliefs embedded in each. One powerful obstacle that North African immigrants face is racial and cultural prejudice. A second major issue is the contrast in gender roles between the old and new cultures, and the differences in family structure and dynamics. Each of these issues is addressed in the novel, as well as the challenge of forging a new identity that accommodates both cultures.

Racial and Cultural Prejudice

As the narrator of *Les Raisins de la galère*, Nadia recounts various incidents occurring within her community that are marked by racial tensions. Each incident powerfully conveys the racial and cultural prejudice faced by immigrants in the imaginary suburb of *Resteville*, and by extension in Arab communities throughout France.

The incident that triggers the narrator's open rebellion against racial discrimination is the destruction of her father's house while she is still a teenager. Her father, a simple mason, has built a beautiful traditional Algerian house in the center of the town. The mayor and his cronies, incensed that an Algerian immigrant could achieve this sort of social stature, order that the family be evicted and the house razed, supposedly so that a community center can be built "for the good of the people."[18] Nadia is outraged by this blatant injustice. As she tells the reader, in her mind, it is a political issue, with racist overtones (21). She continues to fight back, even after her parents give up the struggle (17). Unfortunately, her attempts to involve the press fail because of the Parisian press's indifference to the plight of immigrants (20).

Later in the novel, a group of youngsters steals money from a cash drawer at City Hall during a school field trip. Nadia and her friend Marc, a counselor at the youth center, are summoned to handle the situation. As each child explains his particular motivation for the theft, the common theme that emerges is the lack of self-esteem, frustration, alienation, and anger that the children feel as a result of prejudice against them, largely based on race. One of the boys, Aziz, uses the high unemployment rate among *Maghrébin* youths as his excuse for the theft (37). Since the boys cannot get jobs to earn spending money, they are tempted to steal and assert their worth and independence by defying authority.

Another boy, Momo, speaks of broken dreams and low self-esteem. He would like to be a musician but can't afford to buy a guitar or a harmonica. For him, the theft is also an act of rebellion against his teacher who systematically degrades him by using racial slurs and calling him a dirty Arab (38). The oppression this child feels is both economic and racial. A third child, Rachid, suffers from rejection not only at school but at home as well. As a result, he becomes a gang leader in the neighborhood streets, the only world that accepts him as he is (40).

A more subtle form of racism explored in the novel is the prejudice the *Beurs* harbor against one another, and hence, indirectly against themselves. In the supermarket where Nadia works as a cashier, she witnesses a North African guard brutally beating an Antillean shoplifter. Many of the security guards at the supermarket are from the former French colonies. When they catch one of their own stealing, they are merciless in their punishment. Ben Jelloun points out that the psychology of racism touches everyone and that the victims of racial oppression can be vicious in their prejudice against their own kind as they struggle to establish social dominance. Nadia says of the security guards: "They wanted to show their white boss that they were even more severe than he was" (28). Nadia tries to intervene and loses her job as a result.

However, even Nadia herself is not immune to the racist messages and cultural bias that surround her. For example, she prefers to date French boys. She writes in her journal: "*My first boyfriend is French. I'm glad he's not an Arab*" (22).[19] While Nadia clearly values her cultural heritage as an Algerian and admires her father, her view of Arab boys is a negative one based in part on her own observation of their behavior: "They infuriate me. In school, they do everything in their power to fail; at home, they behave like kings; in the streets, they hang out or hustle" (73). As Nadia struggles to establish her own identity and worth, she is torn between her desire to claim her Algerian heritage and her resentment towards members of her culture who succumb to or even reinforce the negative stereotypes of Algerians in France.

Nadia's Moroccan friend Hamid points out to her that her attitude toward

Arab males is in fact a form of racism. He claims that every Arab male is not like her brother-in-law, and complains that even though, as a political activist, she is always ready to defend Arab rights, she does not accept any of them in her intimacy (68). Self-loathing is one of the most damaging byproducts of racism, as repeatedly expressed in African- American literature. This phenomenon is also particularly well illustrated in another recent francophone work by Marlène Amar entitled *La Femme sans tête* (1993) where a Jewish Algerian woman undergoes a succession of plastic surgery operations to make her body conform to European standards of beauty, to the point of losing her identity and, finally, her life.[20]

In his novel, Ben Jelloun creates a somewhat surreal but profoundly evocative image of the loss of human potential that occurs when the members of a group of people are systematically denigrated and devalued. In an internal tirade that approaches stream of consciousness, Nadia explodes: "We're damned. Not wanted. No purpose, no plan. We're only good as targets for cops and security guards. Whole families are heaped in tidy little piles, then they're forgotten like dirty clothes under the bed" (55). She then imagines a huge stadium where all the *Beurs* would be rounded up, held, and, the image even suggests, exterminated (56). This passage mirrors the rounding up of Jews in a Paris stadium during World War II, prior to their deportation to extermination camps, and subtly but powerfully links these two examples of racist oppression.

Despite this grim warning, Ben Jelloun also uses the novel to explore possible strategies to counteract the destructive power of racism. Nadia's father suggests that the Arabs must take responsibility for their own destiny. They must guard their children from becoming delinquents, drug addicts, drug dealers, or dropouts (63). Building his own home in the center of town is an affirmation of his pride and identity, even if the French authorities eventually destroy his dream.

For Nadia, doing well in school, attending the university, and running for political office as a Green Party candidate constitute powerful attempts to counteract racist stereotypes and explore opportunities for civic participation and social transformation. She refuses to be defined as a second-class citizen and social outcast. Her political activism reflects her determination to become a full, legitimate, and powerful member of society, unlike her silent and oppressed immigrant father.

Nadia becomes the leader of the local chapter of *SOS Racisme*, a national association against racism. And when a local Arab boy, Kamel Mellou, is murdered by the police, she leads the effort to erect a monument in his memory. She explains how Mellou's death touches the entire Arab community. They all feel targeted by his murder and wonder who will be next (55).

Indeed, Nadia appears prepared to single-handedly right all the wrongs done to her people. Her list of tasks to accomplish (not including personal needs like having her hair done) is both ambitious and impressive. It includes granting an interview to *Le Monde*, writing an article for the local newspaper, sitting for a portrait with Harlem Désir,[21] calling a few mayors, arranging an interview with the president, doing a live show for *Radio-Beur*, meeting with two or three foreign correspondents, and calling the association's lawyer to see how the lawsuit against the Front National is progressing (115). She drives herself to the point where she risks complete exhaustion, personal isolation and loneliness. She clearly needs others to support her efforts and to work with her. The whole community needs to get involved in order to create change.

Another strategy for immigrant success is suggested by the character Naima. She is a stunningly beautiful, intelligent girl, the mirror image of Nadia's intellect and physique. She uses her attributes to escape the *Beur* stereotype by becoming a top model for an Italian designer named Arnoldo Benedetto.[22] Her path is quite different from Nadia's because, for her, personal liberation and professional success mean leaving her home community. She chooses a fresh start rather than trying to create change within a community that is permeated by negative cultural stereotypes and a pervasive psychology of failure. Indeed, when she leaves and doesn't return, everyone fears that she has become a prostitute, an all too frequent fate for a *Maghrébin* runaway.

Gender Roles and Family Structure and Dynamics

It is clear from Ben Jelloun's text that *Maghrébin* men have suffered an intense crisis of gender and cultural identity as a result of their immigration/ transplantation into French culture. Nadia's brother-in-law typifies the Arab male at his worst, a man who has never adapted to French ways and who appears as a brute and a good-for-nothing.

The older generation of Arab immigrants is consistently depicted in the novel as worn out and defeated. Nadia's grandfather is a case in point: "France had used him up. The cold that penetrated his bones had consumed him from the inside out" (13). This "cold" symbolizes the physical, emotional, and psychological climate the immigrants find in France.

Many immigrant fathers in present-day France face another problem in that they are no longer granted the traditional authority of the family patriarch. Scorned and disobeyed by their children, and generally devalued by society, they have no way to vent their feelings of impotence and frustration. Eventually, their sense of alienation and displacement within their families and within this new culture, coupled with the physical hardships they endure daily, reduces them to quiet despair. Nadia's father succumbs to depression (32); the Backer father, when all else fails, physically abuses his children. As a child, he had always respected his parents, but as an adult he failed miserably with his children and did not know what to do about it (44); Yamina, Kbira, and Rosa's father imprisons his daughters in Algeria (77–85); and Naima's father would rather believe his daughter dead than face her emancipation (113).

In the case of the younger men, the problem is not one of geographic or cultural displacement since they were all born at the Sarcelles hospital near Paris, as Ben Jelloun points out, not without irony. Nevertheless, they, too, experience anger, despair, and alienation. Unlike their fathers, most of them are unemployed and as a result lack any sense of professional worth or accomplishment. Their unemployment contributes to their lack of self-esteem and their feelings of hopelessness.

At home, on the other hand, they are often shown preferential treatment by their mothers and consequently expect all women to cater to them. The result is a frustrated sense of male superiority and an inability to take action on their own behalves. Nadia's brother Aziz is a good example. He is strong, handsome, smart, and has a real talent for soccer, but never manages to follow through and ends up wasting his potential: "It was his laziness and the image North African boys have of themselves that ruined him, a lack of self-esteem and confidence" (74). He gradually stopped going to practices, started smoking pot, and hanging out with local dropouts. Finally, when Nadia's brother ends up as a Renault factory worker, like their father, the narrator is furious.

One of the rare avenues for positive identity open to these boys is affiliation with the fundamentalist religious movement, the *Front Islamiste du Salut*. For many of them, religion becomes a source of cultural identity and pride. The FIS is also attractive because it supports the return to traditional cultural values, in particular the absolute domination of men over women. Ironically, but perhaps not surprisingly, the cousin Nourredine who joins the cult is in actuality a weak, pitiful young man. The author shows him to be a perfect target. He lets his beard grow, drops out of school, and tries to impose his new way of life at home. He forces his mother and sisters to wear veils and to pray together five times a day. Moreover, he refuses to eat food purchased with money from his father's café where alcohol is served (50). As a result of his conversion, Nourredine creates a living hell for his entire family and ends up dying of malnutrition because he won't touch any "tainted" food. His case illustrates how dangerous such cults can be both for the community and the individual.

In another instance, FIS members try to convince Nadia to involve them in her political campaign, since they also promote *Maghrébin* pride. However, they make it very clear to her at the same time that they do not approve of women running for office or seeking prominence in any other way. Nadia politely rejects their offer of assistance.

Not all the male characters in the novel are failures, however. Two positive, sympathetic, masculine models stand out. They are Nadia's father, an Algerian immigrant, and Marc, her French boyfriend, who believes himself to be part Arab. He is an orphan who does not know his birth parents. Both of these men are strong, gentle, poetic, and unwavering in their struggle to maintain their own dignity and that of others. Nadia's father is her inspiration to speak out and fight for *Maghrébin* rights. Marc offers her the warmth, kindness, and affirmation she needs to continue her efforts.

The fact that Ben Jelloun chooses to address these complex social issues through the voice of a young Algerian woman is significant. He thus gives voice to Arab women who have traditionally been both silent and oppressed. The use of the first person narrative allows the author to explore the character's internal psychology: "The narrative skill that I want to achieve is the ability to climb inside a person and express his or her feelings and emotions. That, in my opinion, is a writer's challenge."[23]

The character Ben Jelloun creates in Nadia is in fact a rebel fighting against both the cultural traditions that oppress women and the negative stereotypes of Arabs in general. Unlike the traditional Arab woman, Nadia refuses to stay at home and limit herself to accepted female roles. She dresses and fights like a boy and dreams of becoming a mechanic when she grows up. This behavior causes her to be rejected by her mother: "She says I'm the man of the house; coming from her, that's not a compliment. She thinks I'm misguided. She's convinced that I'll never be a mother, that I'll never have my own family" (73–74). Despite her mother's fears, Nadia claims both her feminine identity and her right to full participation in society.

Although Nadia dresses and acts like a boy, she copes better than most Arab boys who have either given up, turned to drugs and petty crime, or joined the FIS. Her success in adjusting to her surroundings is consistent with actual sociological studies which indicate that *Beur* women in general adapt more readily to French society than men do.[24] The women do well in school, attend the university, work hard, and get ahead. The men on the other hand, have a much harder time establishing themselves and finding a positive identity.

Nevertheless, the acculturation of Arab women into French society presents its own set of problems. Young Arab girls attend French schools and enjoy freedoms they would not have in Algeria. While Algerian fathers may tolerate this freedom while the girls are small, it is not uncommon for them to try to impose traditional codes of conduct and conventional marriages when the girls reach adolescence. In the text, the story of the three sisters who were kidnapped by their father is a tragic illustration of the difficulties that Arab women face. The father sends his daughters to Algeria and has them sequestered in an Algerian village with his brother for fear that they might turn to prostitution in Paris. The girls write desperately to their friends in France for assistance, and Nadia tries to help. But nothing can be done to circumvent the father's orders and one of the girls finally commits suicide (77–85).

Another example of the difficulty of female acculturation is the situation of Agnès. She is a Paris streetwalker who uses public restrooms to service her clients. Her real name is Bahia. She is an Arab woman who has been physically abused and has run away from home. In her rage and despair, she has turned to prostitution (39). She has changed her name and appearance to make herself more attractive to her customers: "She was a fake blond, with fake eyelashes, fake breasts and a phony name" (38). She illustrates the loss of positive female identity in the transition between the tightly structured role for women in *Maghrébin* culture and the more liberated role that the new culture appears to promise.

The struggle for a new, more liberated identity within French society is a difficult one for Arab women who must fight poverty, abuse, and prejudice merely to survive. Nevertheless, another female character, Naima, manages to find an escape route and an avenue for economic success. The implicit suggestion is that there are opportunities for Arab women in their new culture. Naima moves successfully from a cultural context in which women have to hide their bodies and cover their faces into the world of commercial modeling where her naked body is displayed in all its natural beauty on posters and billboards. In doing so, she demonstrates that the Arab body is beautiful in its own right and that it represents a female form every bit as desirable as the European female. She is the exact opposite of the Algerian Jewish woman in Marlène Amar's *La Femme sans tête*, who mutilates her body in order to conform to a European standard of beauty. Nevertheless, Naima, too, pays a high price for her liberation. Her family and her father in particular are unable to understand or accept her behavior. She is forbidden to ever return home and her family actually refuses to acknowledge that she ever existed. Thus, in attaining fame, success, and a new identity, she is cut off from her family and her home community.

Resolving Cross-Cultural Conflict: Forging a New Identity

The opening paragraph in the novel raises the question of cultural identity and clashing cultural norms with a blunt assertion: "My sister's husband is very much the way we like them in the Arab world. He's cocky, self-satisfied and likes to be waited on. His wife is also his maid" (8). The French "*on les aime*" can be translated either as "*we* like them" or "*they* like them," an interesting translation question, because the narrator situates herself both within and outside Arab culture. When the phrase first appears, Nadia seems to include herself in the *on*, but by the time this same sentence reappears in the text, Nadia has clearly separated herself from the values and expectations of traditional Arab society, and *on* becomes *they*. This shift occurs after she recounts how she was called upon to display the bloodied sheet from her sister's wedding night to prove the bride's virginity to the community.[25]

Toward the end of the novel, Nadia reflects on her own identity when she examines her national ID card and is struck by the fact that no particular mention is made of racial or ethnic features. She reads aloud reflecting: "*special marks: none*. They didn't write anything. Does it mean that I am *nothing*? Not even a 'rebel' or an angry *Beur*" (124). This comment is particularly poignant because of the dual dilemma of *Beur* cultural identity. On the one hand, the *Beurs* would like to be accepted as ordinary full-fledged French citizens, blending into the crowd; but on the other hand, they fear losing their identity, becoming *nothing*, neither Algerian, nor French, nor perhaps even human.[26]

At the very end of the book, which is written in the third person, Ben Jelloun and his heroine appear ready to embrace both Nadia's Arab heritage and her emerging identity in the new culture. The mailman rings at her door, and she signs for a package in Arabic. It seems to amuse the mailman, who then hands her a blank sheet of paper and asks her for an autograph, in admiration: "it's beautiful, the way you write from right to left!" (136). Her *Beur* identity now appears in a positive rather than a negative light. Perhaps she and her generation hold the promise of a new society, full of hybrid vigor and beauty.

The question is no longer whether one belongs to one cultural group or another, but how to take the best from each culture, and to value each for its richness and uniqueness in forging one's identity. Nadia's father's voice prompts her to move forward while never forgetting the past. He urges her to leave the country, travel, and discover the world. But he also admonishes her, wherever she goes, to remember her roots (135). He even gives her permission to embrace a new, more liberated female identity when he says: "you're a free woman. We don't like that too much in our culture, but I always wanted you that way" (135). Nadia's bold signature in Arabic, on the blank sheet of paper, ends the silencing of the past and announces a bright future, the beginning of a new chapter for her and for all Arab immigrants, male and female.

Conclusion

In the end, while Tahar Ben Jelloun forcefully portrays the hardship and despair of immigrant life in modern France (*la galère*), the novel's final message is one of hope and reconciliation (*les raisins*). Ben Jelloun suggests that despite economic hardship and racial intolerance, the *Beurs* will find an identity that combines the best of both cultures. His message is particularly timely in light of the racist politics of the National Front in France, and the reign of terror that is tearing Algeria apart. It serves as a counterpoint to these grave social currents and is worthy of our attention.

NOTES

1. According to Alec G. Hargreaves in *Immigration, 'Race' and Ethnicity in Contemporary France* (NewYork: Routledge, 1995), there are probably three to four million *Maghrébins* currently living in France. There are about 620,000 Algerian, 575,000 Moroccan, and 210,000 Tunisian citizens (1990 census), in addition to about a million and a half to two million French citizens of *Maghrébin* descent (14, 119). In recent times the immigrant population has continued to grow, but, as Alec G. Hargreaves points out, exact figures are almost impossible to obtain.

2. The term *Beur* derives from the word *Arabe* in *verlan*, a popular street language used by young people in France. *Verlan* inverts syllables of existing words to form new slang variations. For example, the word *femme* becomes *meuf*. Ironically, the word *Beur* has now become the common term to designate second generation *Maghrébins*, and a new *verlan* term, *Reub*, has emerged as a slang variation on *Beur*.

3. The Northwest region of North Africa including Algeria, Morocco, and Tunisia. The Kingdom of Morocco (pop. 27 million) and the Republic of Tunisia (pop. 9 million) were French protectorates (Morocco: 1912–1956; Tunisia: 1881–1956); the Republic of Algeria (pop. 28 million) was a French colony (1870–1963).

4. See for example Alec G. Hargreaves: "Research on the representation of minority ethnic groups on French television has shown that they are mainly visible as 'problems' in news and current affairs broadcasts" (158).

5. Tahar Ben Jelloun was kind enough to grant Sylvie Charron an interview in Paris on March 7, 1998. This information was gathered during the interview and is cited with his permission.

6. A partial list of Ben Jelloun's works is given below. Titles of published English translations are in italics, followed by the name of the publisher. English titles for works which have not been published are our own interpretation and should be used with caution.

La Nuit sacrée	*The Sacred Night* (New York: Ballantine, 1991)
L'Enfant de sable	*The Sand Child* (San Diego: Harcourt, Brace, 1987)
Harrouda	Harrouda
Moha le fou, Moha le sage	Moha the Fool, Moha the Wise
La prière de l'absent	The Prayer of the Absent
L'Ecrivain public	The Public Scribe
L'Homme rompu	*Corruption* (New York: New Press, 1995)
La Nuit de l'erreur	The Night of the Error
La Réclusion solitaire	*Solitaire* (London: Quartet, 1988)
Les Yeux baissés	*With Downcast Eyes* (Boston: Little, Brown, 1993)
La Fiancée de l'eau	The Fiancee
Le Premier amour est aussi le dernier	The First Love Is Also the Last

7. For an analysis of *La Réclusion solitaire* and *Les Yeux baissés*, see Brinda Mehta's excellent article, "Alienation, Dispossession, and the Immigrant Experience in Tahar Ben Jelloun's *Les Yeux baissés*," *The French Review* 68.1 (October 1994): 79–91.

8. For a more detailed analysis of Ben Jelloun's works and their place in *Maghrébin* literature, see Jean Déjeux: *La Littérature maghrébine d'expression française*, Paris: P.U.F., 1992.

9. Tahar Ben Jelloun, *Le Racisme expliqué à ma fille* (Paris: Seuil, 1998).

10. The National Front (FN) has been winning a growing share of the national vote, rising from less than 1 percent after its founding in 1972 to 15 percent in the first round of the presidential election in 1995. Furthermore, cities like Orange, Vitrolles, and Toulon are currently run by the National Front and are implementing openly racist policies, illegal by French law (for example denying the *Maghrébins* access to low-income housing, closing employment agencies, banning freedom of speech).

11. The novel's title was inspired by a document on the situation of Arab immigrants in the French suburbs, done by *Banlieuescopies*, a research organization headed by Tahar Ben Jelloun. The original document was already entitled *Les Raisins de la galère*, as a play on words with John Steinbeck's *Les Raisins de la colère* (*The Grapes of Wrath*, New York: Viking, 1939). The word *galère*, which means *galleys*, is commonly used in modern France to designate the hopelessness of life in general. Inadequate schools, unemployment or low-skill jobs, dilapidated housing, broken families, racism, are all part of *la galère*. Ben Jelloun's novel was published in Paris by Fayard, in the collection *Libres*, in 1996.

12. For more information about this law, see Alec G. Hargreaves 169–77.

13. See Yamina Benguigui's documentary, *Mémoires d'immigrés, l'héritage maghrébin* (Cara M., 1998). The film is in three parts, *Les pères, les mères, les enfants*, and depicts the lives of immigrant fathers, mothers, and children (the *Beur* generation), using personal accounts, interviews, and documentary footage. Benguigui's film is educational and intensely moving. She tells the *Maghrébin* story, which has largely been ignored until now.

14. Information gathered from Benguigui's film, *Mémoires d'immigrés: Les Enfants*. She notes that the gatekeepers were sometimes French veterans of the Algerian War, predisposed to treat the immigrants with scorn and disrespect.

15. Slimane Zeghidour, "Le FLN déclenche la guerre d'indépendance," *Géo* 229, March 1998: 95. Cover story on Algeria: 56–131.

16. See Philippe Bernard and Nathaniel Herzberg, *Lettres d'Algérie* (Paris: Gallimard/Le Monde, 1998).

17. Marcus Mabry, "The Triangle of Death: A Futile Attempt to Stop Algeria's Terror," *Newsweek* 23 February 1998: 38. The actual count could be three times that high.

18. Based on an actual incident (author's interview). In the novel, the home is eventually replaced by a small supermarket. As a rule, PCF (communist) voters have been less inclined to favor the politics of the FN than more conservative voters from the UDF or RPR parties (Hargreaves 185).

19. Nadia's journal, and other correspondence in the novel, are printed in italics in the text.

20. See Susan Ireland's article, "Writing the Body in Marlène Amar's *La Femme sans tête*," *The French Review* 71.3 (1998): 454–67.

21. The national leader of *SOS Racisme*.

22. In the previously mentioned interview, Ben Jelloun explains that the character of Naima is entirely a product of his imagination, inspired by a perfume ad, featuring the naked body of a perfectly beautiful woman lying on a sofa. Nevertheless, the Italian designer Louis Benetton, who sponsored a series of scandalous advertising campaigns in Europe, was delighted to find himself represented in barely camouflaged form in the novel. His subsequent

relationship with Ben Jelloun has encouraged him to continue promoting racial tolerance in his advertising.

23. Interview with Ben Jelloun.

24. See for instance Liliane M. Vassberg, "Immigration maghrébine en France: l'intégration des femmes," *The French Review* 70.5 (1997). She indicates that the *Beurettes* have played an important role in changing family dynamics, and that even the mothers have started taking care of family budgets, purchases, and administrative tasks traditionally reserved for the men. However, this has in turn contributed to the disintegration of the traditional *Maghrébin* family structure.

25. One sequence in Benguigui's film relates the pain and shame of an Arab woman when her bloodless wedding sheet was displayed. Her husband had been too drunk to perform. In the novel, Nadia does not bleed when she loses her virginity to Marc. She assumes her hymen has been torn during her frequent sports activities. She, too, would have been unfairly shamed if her wedding sheet had been displayed in the traditional manner.

26. A similar psychology surfaces in Frédérique Chevillot's interview, "Beurette suis et beurette ne veux pas toujours être: entretien avec Tassadit Imache," *The French Review* 71.4 (1998): 645–50. Even though Tassadit Imache has a French passport and a French mother, she feels deeply connected to her father, an Algerian immigrant, and can't decide what her "true" identity is.

REFERENCES

Amar, Marlène. *La Femme sans tête*. Paris: Gallimard, 1993.

Ben Jelloun, Tahar. *Corruption*. New York: New Press, 1995.

——. *L'Ecrivain public*. Paris: Seuil, 1983.

——. *L'Enfant de sable*. Paris: Seuil, 1985.

——. *La Fiancée de l'eau*, théâtre, suivi de *Entretiens avec M. Said Hammadi, ouvrier Algérien*. Paris: Actes Sud, 1984.

——. *Harrouda*. Paris: Denoel, 1973.

——. *L'Homme rompu*. Paris: Seuil, 1994.

——. "Ma Mère ne viendra pas en France." *Le Monde* 18 April 1997: 8.

——. *Moha le fou, Moha le sage*. Paris: Seuil, 1978.

——. *La Nuit de l'erreur*. Paris: Seuil, 1997.

——. *La Nuit sacrée*. Paris: Seuil, 1987.

——. Personal Interview with Sylvie Charron. 7 March 1998.

——. *Le Premier amour est aussi le dernier*. Paris: Seuil, 1995.

——. *La Prière de l'absent*. Paris: Seuil, 1981.

——. *Le Racisme expliqué à ma fille*. Paris: Seuil, 1998.

——. *Les Raisins de la galère*. Paris: Fayard, 1996.

——. *La Réclusion solitaire*. Paris: Seuil, 1973.

——. *The Sacred Night*. New York: Ballantine, 1991.

——. *The Sand Child*. San Diego: Harcourt, Brace, 1987.

——. *Solitaire*. London: Quartet, 1988.

——. *With Downcast Eyes*. Boston: Little, Brown, 1993.

——. *Les Yeux baissés*. Paris: Seuil, 1991.

Benguigui, Yamina, dir. *Mémoires d'immigrés, l'héritage maghrébin*. Cara M., 1998.

Bernard, Philippe, and Nathaniel Herzberg. *Lettres d'Algérie*. Paris: Gallimard/Le Monde, 1998.

Chevillot, Frédérique. "Beurette suis et beurette ne veux pas toujours être: entretien avec Tassadit Imache." *The French Review* 71.4 (1998): 645–50.

Déjeux, Jean. *La Littérature maghrébine d'expression française*. Paris: Presses Universitaires de France, 1992.

Hargreaves, Alec G. *Immigration, 'Race' and Ethnicity in Contemporary France*. New York: Routledge, 1995.

Ireland, Susan. "Writing the Body in Marlène Amar's *La Femme sans tête*." *The French Review* 71.3 (1998): 454–67.

Kassovitz, Mathieu, dir. *La Haine (Hate)*. 1995.

Mabry, Marcus. "Triangle of Death: A Futile Attempt to Stop Algeria's Terror." *Newsweek* 23 February 1998: 38.

Mehta, Brinda. "Alienation, Dispossession, and the Immigrant Experience in Tahar Ben Jelloun's *Les Yeux baissés*." *The French Review* 68.1 (October 1994): 79–91.

Steinbeck, John. *The Grapes of Wrath*. New York: Viking, 1939.

Vassberg, Liane, Mi: "Immigration maghrébine en France: l'intégration des femmes." *French Review* 70.5 (1997): 710–20.

Zeghidour, Slimane. "Le FLN déclenche la guerre d'indépendance." *Géo* 229, March 1998: 56–131.
Zemmouri, Mahmoud, dir. *100% Arabica.* 1997.

DISCUSSION QUESTIONS

1. What images do you have of the *Beur* generation after reading this chapter? What similarities and differences do you see between their circumstances and the situation of various racial and ethnic groups in the United States?

2. Compare the identity struggles of the *Beurs* with similar situations in the USA that you might be familiar with, for example with *latinos*, or other immigrant groups.

3. What forms of action does Nadia take to defend the rights of immigrants? What forms of political and social action can help ensure the rights of immigrants or minorities in the USA?

4. Compare Ben Jelloun's presentation with Mathieu Kassovitz's film *La Haine*, or Mahmoud Zemmouri's *100% Arabica*, which also depict life in the *banlieues*. What similarities and/or differences do you see in the presentation of the suburban housing projects?

5. Why does Ben Jelloun make metaphoric references to the Jewish holocaust in the novel? What parallels exist between the racism currently endured by the Arabs in modern France and the Jewish experience during World War II?

6. How do the tensions between the old and new cultures play out in terms of gender roles, and family structure and dynamics? Consider the *Beurs* and/or other immigrant groups that you are familiar with.

7. What role does religion (in this case, Islam) play in affirming cultural identity? Explore specific examples.

8. Can a male writer effectively convey the voice and experience of a female character, and vice-versa? What are the difficulties? You may use Tahar Ben Jelloun as an example, or use other texts that you are familiar with.

9. Would you consider Nadia to be a feminist? Why or why not?

10. What are the cultural origins of your family and in what ways has that cultural heritage shaped who you are? You may address issues of national origin, language, race, gender, class, and religion.

PART THREE

Francophone Issues in the Caribbean

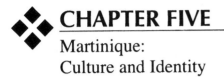

CHAPTER FIVE
Martinique:
Culture and Identity

Debra L. Anderson

Like many visitors, on my first trip to Martinique, I was impressed by its "Frenchness." Having lived in France for two years, I quickly recognized signs and landmarks that dotted the urban landscape near my hotel in Fort de France: from the *bureau de poste* (post office) on the rue de la Liberté to the small *boulangerie* (bakery) near my hotel, it seemed as if part of France had been transplanted to this small Caribbean island. One of my first meals seemed to confirm this "Frenchness": at a small cafe, I enjoyed a late lunch of the only remaining item on the menu, *boeuf bourgignon*—a very traditional French beef stew made with red wine. However, there was something a little different and not quite "French" about the meal: it was served not with the typical potatoes but with a purée of *ignames*—a root vegetable served throughout the Caribbean. I began to question my initial impression of the island's "Frenchness."

In an essay on Martinique, the Trinidadian author, V. S. Naipaul, observes that crossing the Caribbean to travel from Trinidad to Martinique is more like crossing the English Channel and arriving in France:

> Martinique is France. . . . The policemen are French; the street nameplates in blue-and-white enamel are French; the cafés are French; the menus are French and are written in a French hand. . . . Unlike the other islands, which have one main town to which everything gravitates, Martinique is full of little French villages, each with its church, *Mairie* and war memorial . . . .(The Middle Passage 211)

Martinique is, in a very real way, French. Colonized by the French in 1635, the island became an overseas department of France—*département d'outre mer*—after World War II in 1946.[1] The island's nearly 400,000 inhabitants are citizens of France with the same rights and benefits as French citizens living in mainland France, or as commonly referred to on the island, the *métropole*.[2] Though somewhat dated, Naipaul's observation of postcolonial Martinique still holds true. What impresses him the most is the success of the French colonial system in assimilating the island's people: "In this society only education and cultured Frenchness matter"(217). French is the official language of the island: business is conducted in French; street nameplates and menus are in French. But on the menu one might find next to the *boeuf bourgignon* a *colombo* (a dish of curried chicken, pork, or goat). This "national dish" of Martinique reflects an influence of workers from India who came to Martinique after the abolition of slavery in the French colonies in 1848. French is not the only language spoken as French Creole — a language born of the plantation system and slavery with both African and European roots — is also widely used. Most of the island's popular music is in French Creole. The island is still "full of little villages"; however, the present consumer economy gravitates around the capital city of Fort de France and the *zone industriel* where a shopping center and discount stores are located.

An important point, as stressed by Naipaul, is that the majority (90%) of the island's population is black, or of mixed African and European heritage. However, to identify the island and its people as French and black oversimplifies the complex question of culture and identity in Martinique. This essay will focus on the question of "identity" in Martinique including a discussion of the predominant literary movements or currents of thought: Négritude (Negritude), Antillanité (Caribbeanness), and Créolité (Creoleness).

Négritude

Influenced by the works of Afro-Cuban, Haitian, and African-American writers (Arnold 26–28), the Négritude movement was founded in Paris during the 1930s. Négritude seeks to defend and rehabilitate black and African cultural values and restore dignity to a race of people oppressed by centuries of slavery and colonization. Its founders, representatives from French colonies in Africa and the New World — Aimé Césaire from Martinique, Léopold Senghor from Senegal, and Léon Gontran Damas from French Guiana — met as students in Paris and founded the journal *L'Etudiant noir* in 1934. Négritude is the black writer's quest for an authentic identity that involves restoring wholeness to a shattered collective cultural and historical identity. "Who and what are we? Admirable question!" is the urgent question posed by Césaire in his seminal work *Cahier d'un retour au pays natal* (*Return to My Native Land*), written in 1939. Négritude is the search for a lost African past and an attempt to restore unity and continuity with the cultural motherland, Africa (as opposed to the "colonial" motherland France). Césaire characterized Négritude as *le grand cri nègre* — the great black cry of revolt against oppression and prejudice. However, according to the French writer and existentialist philosopher, Jean-Paul Sartre, the black poet, in his revolt against oppression and prejudice, speaks for all colonized and oppressed people — Négritude's "cry" was universal: "The black man who is conscious of himself sees himself as the man who has taken the whole of human suffering upon himself and who suffers for all, even the white man" (Sartre 320).

In his preface to the first anthology of black poetry in French, "Black Orpheus,"[3] Sartre described the writers and the movement in terms of his existentialist philosophy while comparing the Négritude writer's search for his "black substance or essence" to Orpheus' descent into hell in search of his lost Eurydice. Sartre and the French surrealist, André Breton,[4] praised the work of these writers who brought new meaning and life to French poetry. They discovered in these poets the embodiment of their theories and a vivacity and force absent from European poetry of the period. Thomas Melone, in his text *De la négritude dans la littérature négro-africaine* (1962), describes the Négritude movement in terms of Sartrean existentialism. The black writer "situates himself in relation to history and space, he becomes conscious of what he is . . . what he wants to become. He refuses his state of 'being a thing,' of being nothing, and affirms his existence. 'I want to be therefore I am.' A veritable cry of hope" (Melone 25). Césaire stated that Breton and surrealism brought a confidence to the literary projects of his generation. In the principles of surrealism, Négritude sought, through the liberation of the unconscious, liberation from the dominant culture: "It [surrealism] provided a tempting solution to the problems of political and most importantly psychological liberation from the metropolitan culture" (Dash, *Literature and Ideology* 157). Furthermore, as Dash states, surrealism "shunned the fatigued rationality and inhibiting materialism of the West and actively promoted the search for spontaneity and originality in non-Western traditions . . . and responded to their specific artistic as well as political needs" (*Literature and Ideology* 157).

Primarily, then, Négritude reveals itself as the poetic expression of the black writer's anti-colonialist revolt. The very foundation of Négritude and the process of rehabilitation and restoration imply the systematic denial of an imposed French system of values which held "temporarily captive an 'African' or 'Black' substance or essence which it was the task of Négritude . . . to release and bring to fruition" (Burton, "The Idea of Difference" 141).

The Négritude poets will emphasize the importance of the culture and traditions of the ancestral homeland—Africa—by a symbolic return. The common theme of "return" is expressed, for example, in the poem "Blues" by Léon Gontran Damas, in which the poet mourns his lost African heritage.[5] This sense of loss is rooted in the "historical experience of slavery: the moment when Africans were captured and sold into slavery: the moment of dispossession and uprooting, which deprived a race of its rightful inheritance" (Ormerod, *Introduction* 1). In the poem "They Came That Night," Damas also conveys the violence of this uprooting: the pain of being torn away from everything familiar. In "Hiccups," the poet no longer focuses on this first painful separation but on the cultural alienation he must endure in a white-dominated society.

For the Senegalese poet, Senghor, the cultural importance of Africa permeates his poetry, but in a more nostalgic and meditative tone (Kennedy 124). In "French Garden," Senghor opposes the noise of the city with the soothing rhythmic sounds of his ancestral homeland. In "Totem," he laments his ancestor or the "totem"—the poet's true cultural heritage and identity—that must remain hidden underneath the veneer of cultural assimilation. This alienation is perhaps most poignantly expressed in the famous poem, "Betrayal" by Haitian poet Léon Laleau who tries to articulate the poet's sense of "betrayal" to this "African" self through poetry written in French—the language of the colonizer, the "master's" language.

Perhaps the most important aspect of Négritude is, as Edouard Glissant states in *Le Discours Antillais* (*Caribbean Discourse*), its power to unify and reunite a population dispersed and dispossessed by colonization:

> Colonization has divided into English, French, Dutch, Spanish territories a region where the majority of the population is African: making strangers out of people who are not. The thrust of negritude among Caribbean intellectuals was a response, perhaps to the need, by relating to a common origin, to rediscover unity (equilibrium) beyond dispersion.[6]

Négritude, however, in its struggle to restore unity and dignity to an oppressed people, did not take into account different cultural, social, and historical realities. The focus of Négritude turned toward a distant and phantom Africa. In the words of the Martinican intellectual René Ménil, one of the first writers to formulate the idea of a West Indian or Caribbean specificity (Burton, "The Idea of Difference" 146), it is "blind to the Caribbean whose islands disappear before our eyes at the command of imperialisms" (Ménil 48). The Martinican poet, essayist, novelist, Edouard Glissant rejected the racial confines of Négritude to become the most important voice in articulating the complexities of a Caribbean identity.

Antillanité

Formulated between the years 1957 and 1958 (Antoine 359), Antillanité, like Négritude is a continuing search for identity. Unlike Négritude, Antillanité has not coalesced into a single movement, thereby contributing, according to Richard D. E. Burton to both its strength as well as its weakness: "Its strength—and also perhaps its weakness—is that virtually everyone in contemporary Martinique . . . proclaims the 'specificity' of French West Indian culture and French West Indian psyche" ("The Idea of Difference" 147). Glissant articulates most thoroughly his concept of Antillanité in his seminal work, *Le Discours Antillais* (*Caribbean Discourse*), first published in 1982: Antillanité is grounded in Caribbean culture and history and in the *questioning* of these cultural and historical realities:

The notion of Antillanité, or Caribbeanness, emerges from a reality that we will have to question, but also corresponds to a dream that we must clarify and whose legitimacy must be demonstrated. A fragile reality (the experience of Caribbeanness, woven together from one side of the Caribbean to the other), negativity twisted together in its urgency (Caribbeanness is a dream, forever denied, often deferred, yet a strange, stubborn presence in our responses). (*CD* 221)

The Caribbean universe is one born of the Plantation System, a common cultural and historical base shared by the islands:

Cultures derived from plantations; . . . social pyramids with an African or East Indian base and a European peak; languages of compromise; general cultural phenomenon of creolization; pattern of encounter and synthesis; persistence of the African presence; cultivation of sugarcane, corn, and pepper; site where rhythms combined; people formed by orality. (*CD* 222)

Antillanité constitutes a complex ensemble of geographic, cultural, and linguistic specificities; shared components, which, in Glissant's vision, unite the Caribbean. Caribbean society is born of a cultural *métissage*—mixing—of people of diverse ethnic origins all of which contribute to its identity and reality. Antillanité, therefore, rejects the simplifying opposition of "African/European" and "Black/White" as set up by Négritude.

Glissant's view of Caribbean history is essential to the concept of Antillanité. Glissant characterizes the Caribbean, and in particular his native Martinique, as an example of a land and a people deprived of their true history. Martinique suffers from what Glissant calls an imposed "nonhistory," that essentially destroyed the collective memory:

The French Caribbean is the site of a history characterized by ruptures and that began with a brutal dislocation, the slave trade. . . . This dislocation of the continuum, and the inability of the collective consciousness to absorb it all, characterize what I call a nonhistory. (*CD* 61–62)

It is the writer's task, through a "prophetic vision of the past," to restore continuity to this disrupted chronology: "Glissant's intent is to recover the lost past of islands whose African heritage has been overshadowed by the trauma of slavery and whose history reveals significant gaps" (Mortimer 65). Glissant does not seek to simply revise or rewrite history: the writer must question and reveal this tormented past and bring to light Martinique's present state of cultural, political, and psychological enslavement. In his novels, Glissant explores the hidden and unwritten history of his homeland in order to reestablish continuity between the past, present, and future. In the process, he restores a consciousness of this historical continuity to his people: "The language of the Caribbean artist does not originate in the obsession of celebrating his inner self; this inner self is inseparable from the future of his community" (*CD* 236).

La Lézarde (*The Ripening*) is Glissant's first of a series of novels in which
he explores the complexities of Martinican history, landscape, and people.[7]
Through his poetry and fiction, Glissant seeks not "merely to relive or reconstruct
the history of the Martinican people but . . . to deliver the island-department's
past . . . from the layers of repression and oblivion in which nearly three and a
half centuries of metropolitan dominance have enshrouded it" (Burton, "Comment peut-on être martiniquais?" 301). The action involves a group of young
political activists campaigning for a progressive candidate. Garin, a reactionary
government official, who plans to build a house at the source of the Lézarde
river, poses a threat not only to the election but to the community: "His desire
to control the spring where the river rises explicitly indicates his determination
to restrict the people's activities" (Dash, "Introduction" 10). The group acts
for the community and decides to assassinate Garin. Through their collective
political act, young people from diverse groups and parts of the island (the city,
the mountain, the plain) act as one and take it upon themselves to change the
course of events—to act upon the island's history—by eliminating the threat
posed by Garin and thus freeing the waters and liberating the land and people.
The protagonist's attempt to "right/write" history is inextricably bound to the
quest for identity. History is central to identity for Glissant.

In *La Lézarde*, Glissant introduces many concepts that he will continue
to develop in his later novels. Papa Longoué, a pivotal recurring character, is
a descendant of the *marrons*—maroon slaves who escaped the plantation to
live in freedom in the *mornes*, or mountains. He represents a vital link with
the island's past and *le pays d'avant*—the land before—Africa. The *morne*
becomes the locus of freedom and resistance in Glissant's novels. *Le paysage*,
the "landscape," plays a crucial role in the characters' collective search for
identity as it is through their search for identity that the characters arrive at a
new understanding of the land. Glissant links the land or landscape to cultural
and historical identity and the "four centuries" of the island's history: "The sea
that you cross is one century. . . . And the coast where, blind, you disembark,
without soul or voice, is one century. And the forest . . . is one century. And
the land, flattened and denuded little by little, is one century" (*Le Quatrième
siècle* 268–69). Glissant's Antillanité involves much more than a "revision" of
the Caribbean's history. Glissant strives to bring a new cultural and historical
awareness to his people. Antillanité is the foundation upon which Glissant will
build his *poétique de la relation*—"cross-cultural poetics"—and in which a new
generation of Martinican writers will find inspiration to continue to explore the
complex question of identity.

Créolité

Eloge de la Créolité (In Praise of Creoleness),[8] a cultural and literary manifesto, is the collective effort of a new generation of Martinican writers who follow in the footsteps of Césaire and Glissant by exploring Martinican cultural and historical identity. Jean Bernabé, Patrick Chamoiseau, and Raphael Confiant represent a generation of writers who have "no direct personal experience of pre-departmental Martinique" (Burton, "Debrouya pas péche" 481). Créolité is the "recognition of the islands' racial diversity; an effort to validate traditional oral culture; an affirmation of the importance of history" (Ormerod, "French West Indian Writing since 1970" 181). *Eloge de la Créolité* is the proclamation of the authors' "acceptance" of their identity and a new stage in their quest for identity. The essay begins, "We declare ourselves Creoles," and they define "Creoleness" as the combination of Caribbean, European, African, and Asian cultural elements that have been brought together by history ("PC" 891). The authors refuse all racial designations to describe their multiracial and multicultural society created by the bringing together of peoples from Europe, Africa, and Asia. They reclaim and redefine the term "Creole," used originally to refer to a person born and raised in the Americas; later, it was mistakenly applied to only white Creoles ("PC" 906).[9] With Négritude and Antillanité as their foundation, Bernabé, Chamoiseau, and Confiant articulate their vision of Créolité or Creoleness. They pay tribute to their predecessors by situating themselves in a literary continuum with Césaire and Glissant. Négritude is, according to the authors, a first important step toward defining a true Caribbean identity because it restores dignity to Africa as the cultural motherland and brings to the Caribbean "its African dimension" ("PC" 888). However, Négritude, like the imposed Frenchness against which it fought, looked outward or externally for affirmation: "the exteriority of aspirations (to mother Africa, mythical Africa, impossible Africa) and the exteriority of self-assertion (we are Africans)" ("PC" 288). In its universality, Négritude reached toward an impossible and unattainable Africa and failed to respond to the unique situation of Caribbean realities.

The writers continue to trace their literary roots through Edouard Glissant whose concept of Antillanité empowered them to refuse "the trap of Négritude" by looking inward toward the Caribbean. Créolité is in essence a continuation of Glissant's concept of Antillanité and, like Antillanité, it emphasizes the complex nature of French Caribbean cultural identity (Burton, "The Idea of Difference" 152). Antillanité allows the writers to escape the imposed European or African space and place themselves within a Caribbean space located firmly in the "Americas." By transcending the universal nature of Négitude's cry of revolt, the writers can truly begin their necessary task: "the minute exploration of ourselves" ("PC" 890). But Créolité does not limit itself to the Caribbean or the Americas. Through their Creoleness, the authors situate themselves in relation to the world by aligning themselves with other multicultural and multiracial societies where multiple cultural elements have been united through the course of history. From the Caribbean to Africa, from Guyana to Polynesia, the writers praise all Creole societies born of the mixing of cultures "which all result from the matrix of the same historical maelstrom" ("PC" 894). Créolité defies racial descriptions and validates the new being created from this chaotic beginning: "To be Creole is to be a compromise between black and white, between black and Indian. . . . This mixture has created a new race, a new language [that is] supple and serpentine . . . " (Confiant, *Le Nègre et l'amiral* 128).

Bernabé, Chamoiseau, and Confiant reestablish the Creole language and culture as the cornerstone of their identity and "the initial means of communicating our deep self, or our collective unconscious" ("PC" 899). In Chamoiseau and Confiant's novels, the Creole language and oral tradition are a vital force.[10] In *Solibo Magnifique* (1989),[11] the plot centers around the Creole storyteller, Solibo, who, like the *conteurs* of the days of slavery speaks to and for the people:

> Our stories and our Storytellers date from the period of slavery and colonialism. Their deepest meanings can be understood only in relation to this fundamental period in the history of the West Indies. Our Storyteller speaks for a people enchained: starving, terrorized, living in the cramped postures of survival. (Chamoiseau xii)

Solibo dies mysteriously in front of his small group of faithful listeners. His death represents the end of the story (the symbolic death of Creole language) and the imposed separation of the community. The official investigation that follows disperses Solibo's audience with often dire consequences. The fact that Chamoiseau includes himself as a character within the novel emphasizes the active role of the writer in bringing a voice to his people. As Ti Cham, Chamoiseau acts as scribe and attempts to record the words of Solibo to preserve them for future generations. But, ultimately, Solibo's words, and the language and cultural traditions he represents, can only be saved by the community. At the end of the novel the community is brought back together, with a renewed sense of identity, reunited by Solibo's words (*les dits de Solibo*) that they reconstitute and bring back to life through their remembrance (Anderson 61). Thus, through the community's action the threatened Creole language and culture survive.

Conclusion

Négritude, Antillanité, and Créolité illustrate the role of the writer in bringing a voice and historical consciousness to a people. In a very real way, these writers effect change by bringing a new cultural awareness to their community. To this end, Glissant formed the *Institut martiniquais d'études*. Today, the Créolité movement has revitalized Creole language and culture. The writer's work is "part of the lived reality of the people. . . . This conscious research creates the possibility of a collective effervescence. If he more or less succeeds, he makes critical thought possible; if he succeeds completely, he can inspire" (*CD* 235–36).

NOTES

1. French Guiana and Guadeloupe also became French overseas departments after World War II. See also Marcia G. Parker and Beverley G. David's essay in this book.

2. According to the *CIA World Factbook* (online), the estimated population of the island in 1996 was 399,151.

3. Sartre's essay is the preface to *Anthologie de la nouvelle poésie nègre et malgache*, the first anthology of black poetry published in 1948 and edited by Léopold Senghor.

4. André Breton's introduction to Césaire's *Cahier d'un retour au pays natal* was first published in the journal *Tropiques* in 1944.

5. The poems referred to in this study are from the anthology *The Negritude Poets*, a selection of poems edited by Ellen Conroy Kennedy.

6. The English version, which is cited here, was translated by J. Michael Dash and was published by the University of Virginia Press in 1989. The English translation contains the bulk of the original text. Selected essays have been omitted from the English translation. All further citations of this text will be indicated by *CD*.

7. The most recent and authoritative translation of *La Lézarde* is *The Ripening* by J. Michael Dash.

8. The original French text was published in 1989 and the English translation appeared in the journal *Callaloo* in 1990. All further citations of the English translation will be indicated by "PC."

9. The definition of "creole" is a much debated and often controversial issue. It was used at one time to designate a person of European heritage who was born in the New World. As these writers point out, it has taken on other meanings historically. In this essay, the authors reclaim the word and use it to describe cultures created from the joining of two or more very different cultures. In the Caribbean and Latin America this "mixing over the centuries has produced a racial spectrum and cultural kaleidoscope whose great variety and richness expresses itself in many ways including language" (Winn 21). On many of the Caribbean islands, a Creole patois or dialect is spoken in addition to the official European language.

10. Confiant's first novels were written in French Creole and both Confiant and Chamoiseau incorporate the Creole language and culture in their novels in French. For a more detailed study of the development of the French Caribbean novel, see Beverly Ormerod's essay "French West Indian Literature since 1970." For a detailed study of the use of Creole in Chamoiseau's novels, see "Débrouya pa péché, or il y a toujours moyen de moyenner" by Richard D. E. Burton.

11. Chamoiseau's third novel, *Texaco* (published in French in 1992), is the only one that has been published in English.

REFERENCES

Anderson, Debra L. *Decolonizing the Text: Glissantian Readings in African-American and Caribbean Literatures.* New York: Peter Lang, 1995.

Antoine, Régis. *La littérature franco-antillaise.* Paris: Khartala, 1992.

Arnold, A. James. *Modernism and Negritude: The Poetry and Poetics of Aimé Césaire.* Cambridge: Harvard University Press, 1981.

Bernabé, Jean, Patrick Chamoiseau, and Raphaël Confiant. *Eloge de la Créolité.* Paris: Gallimard, 1989.

Breton, André. "Martinique charmeuse de serpents: un grand poète noir." *Tropiques* 11 (1944).

Burton, Richard D. E. "Comment peut-on être martiniquais: The Recent Work of Edouard Glissant." *Modern Language Review* 79.2 (1984): 301–12.

——. "Débrouya pa péché, or il y a toujours moyen de moyenner: Patterns of Opposition in the Fiction of Patrick Chamoiseau." *Callaloo* 16.2 (1993): 466–81.

——. Fred Reno, and A. James Arnold, eds. *French and West Indian: Martinique, Guadeloupe, and French Guiana Today.* Charlottesville: University of Virginia Press, 1995.

——. "The Idea of Difference in Contemporary West Indian Thought." *French and West Indian: Martinique, Guadeloupe, and French Guiana Today.* Charlottesville: University of Virginia Press, 1995. 137–66.

Césaire, Aimé. *Cahier d'un retour au pays natal.* 1947. Paris: Présence Africaine, 1971.

CIA World Factbook. Online. 1996.

Chamoiseau, Patrick. *Creole Folktales.* Trans. Linda Coverdale. New York: New Press, 1994.

——. *Solibo Magnifique.* Paris: Gallimard, 1988.

——. *Texaco.* Trans. Rose Myriam Réjouis and Val Vinokurov. New York: Pantheon, Books, 1997.

Confiant, Raphaël. *Le Nègre et l'amiral.* Paris: Grasset, 1989.

Dash, J. Michael. Introduction. *The Ripening.* By Edouard Glissant. London: Heinemann, 1981.

——. *Literature and Ideology in Haiti: 1915–1961.* Totowa, NJ: Barnes and Noble Books, 1981.

Glissant, Edouard. *Caribbean Discourse.* Trans. J. Michael Dash. Charlottesville: University of Virginia Press, 1989.

——. *Le discours antillais.* Paris: Editions du Seuil, 1981.

——. *La Lézarde.* Paris: Editions du Seuil, 1958.

——. *Le Quatrième siècle.* Paris: Editions du Seuil, 1964.

Kennedy, Ellen Conroy, ed. *The Negritude Poets.* New York: Viking Press, 1975.

Melone, Thomas. *De la négritude dans la littérature négro-africaine.* Paris: Présence Africaine, 1962.

Ménil, René. *Tracées: Identité, négritude, esthétique aux Antilles.* Paris: Editions Robert Laffont, 1981.

Naipaul, V. S. *The Middle Passage.* New York: MacMillan, 1963.

Ormerod, Beverly. "Beyond Negritude: Some Aspects of the Work of Edouard Glissant." *Contemporary Literature* 15.3 (1974): 360–69.

——. "Discourse and Dispossession: Glissant's Image of Contemporary Martinique." *Caribbean Quarterly* 27.4 (1981): 1–12.

——. "French West Indian Writing Since 1970." *French and West Indian: Martinique, Guadeloupe, and French Guiana Today.* Charlottesville: University of Virginia Press, 1995. 167–87.

——. *An Introduction to the French Caribbean Novel.* London: Heinemann, 1985.

Senghor, L. S., ed. *Anthologie de la nouvelle poésie nègre et malgache de langue française.* Paris: Presses Universitaires de France, 1948.

——. "Black Orpheus." Trans. Jack MacCombie. *"What Is Literature?" and Other Essays.* Ed. Steven Ungar. Cambridge: Harvard University Press, 1988. 291–330.

Winn, Peter. *Americas: The Changing Face of Latin America and the Caribbean.* New York: Pantheon Books, 1992.

DISCUSSION QUESTIONS

1. What was the primary objective of the Négritude poets? How did they achieve this in their writings?

2. Discuss the importance of Africa for the Négritude poets. Why do Bernabé, Chamoiseau, and Confiant consider Africa "impossible"?

3. Why do Bernabé, Chamoiseau, and Confiant characterize Négritude as the "exteriority of asprirations" and the "exteriority of self-assertion"?

4. According to Glissant, what is the role of the writer?

5. Both Antillanité and Créolité refuse the racial confines of Négritude. Why? How do these movements (concepts) differ from Négritude?

CHAPTER SIX
Staging Decolonization:
The Theater of Aimé Césaire

Timothy Scheie

Aimé Césaire enjoys an international reputation as both a poet and a statesman, or more accurately a poet *as* statesman, for the motivation behind his political positions often finds its most eloquent expression in his poetry. His conception of black identity in a colonial world, *negritude*, generates the power of works such as *Notebook of a Return to My Native Land* and fuels his advocacy of Martiniquais interests as a deputy to the French National Assembly. He is arguably less recognized as a playwright. Although his dramatic *œuvre* has garnered the attention of readers and spectators worldwide, it is often received as either an inflection of his politics or a continued expression of his poetic vision; it is rarely considered in terms of theatrical practice itself (Livingston 182). Nevertheless, Césaire's ability to reveal the complexity of the (post-)colonial struggle for identity and autonomy in these plays cannot be dissociated from his self-conscious appropriation of theatrical tradition. A profound sense of spectacle inhabits his dramatic writings, and his use of masks, song, ceremony, and other theatrical devices gives his poetry a voice and brings the political message to the spectator.

Césaire's dramatic production coincides with a crucial period in colonial history. His three major plays, *The Tragedy of King Christophe* (1963), *A Season in the Congo* (1965), and *A Tempest* (1968), were produced at a time when many former colonies were achieving independence and faced thorny questions of national, cultural, and racial identity. Césaire's own Martinique, it should be noted, did not win independence, but instead became an overseas *département* of France. Césaire led the campaign for departmenthood, a position for which he later expressed a certain amount of regret. His plays betray a similar hesitancy to advocate a single, "correct" course of action, and raise many questions. What will these nascent national identities mean? How does one live one's new identity as, for example, a Senegalese or a Congolese? What form of government will replace the colonial system? Will it be modeled on European governments, or take a radically different turn? How will the many ethnicities that inhabit these countries get along? How will the deeply rooted notions of racial identity inflect in the new political climate? These questions preoccupy Césaire's plays, and all three address the painful process of decolonization. However, they do not furnish facile solutions, nor do they preach a particular party line. Instead, they represent the characters' attempts to negotiate a viable national and racial identity in a complex postcolonial world. Just as history has not yet settled these questions, as the recent conflicts in Haiti, the Democratic Republic of Congo (formerly Zaïre), and various central African nations attest, the open-endedness of Césaire's dramatic works likewise leaves the spectator to ponder possible resolutions to the conflicts on the stage. These plays will surely disappoint the spectator who seeks easy answers to the postcolonial dilemma.

To represent the complexities of decolonization, Césaire chose not to follow the familiar conventions of dramatic realism. Instead, he sought inspiration in the theories of German playwright and theorist Bertolt Brecht (1898–1956). Brechtian "epic" theater rejects the tenets of mimetic or Aristotelian theater that underlie much Western theater practice, namely, that the spectator identify with the characters and view the stage as a more or less "realistic" and therefore "true" representation of both reality and the human condition. In conventional Western drama, even if the particulars of the character's situation are different from those of the spectator, on a universal level the action is "realistic"; the spectators relate to the emotions and plights of, say, a matricidal Greek prince such as Orestes, although they themselves might live in the twentieth century and come from a functional and loving family. Instead of trying to make a situation so outlandish and extreme seem realistic and believable, Brecht took the opposite tack: to make the familiar seem strange and surprising, to make the most apparently logical and "realistic" events seem amazing and contradictory. Rather than appealing to the spectator's idea of "reality," Brecht sought to show that it is historical and therefore *changeable*. Brecht firmly believed that a specific social and historical context determines an individual's idea of what it means to be "human," and rejected the idea that such a transcendent, transhistorical, universal humanity eclipses differences of historical period and place. One might add differences of social class, age, race and gender to this list, although one should be aware that both Brecht's and Césaire's representations of gender have drawn criticism.

Césaire's plays bear the clear mark of Brechtian theory. The first visit of Brecht's Berliner Ensemble to Paris in 1954 shook up the French theater world, and provoked heated discussions between supporters and detractors of his theater. Many French directors drew inspiration from this provocative, revolutionary esthetic. One of these, Jean-Marie Serreau, would eventually direct all three of Césaire's plays, and worked closely with Césaire in preparing the final versions of these plays for production; indeed, Serreau is indissociably linked to the development of Césaire's dramaturgy and his reputation as a playwright. However, a less circumstantial, more philosophical affinity also links Brecht and Césaire.

Like Brecht, Césaire also sought to alienate and reveal the contradictory logic of a given historical moment, that of decolonization. Césaire's formulation of negritude as the historical and cultural nature of racial identity differs from that of other francophone poets, most notably Léopold Sédar Senghor, who insist on the biological roots of their negritude. In marked contrast, Césaire refused to recognize a racial identity that exists beyond the historical contingencies of the present. Césaire's negritude is not ontologically or biologically fixed, but a dynamic identity under negotiation as history unfolds before it: "My negritude is grounded. It's a fact that there is black culture: it's historical, it has nothing biological" (*Magazine Littéraire*, my translation). There is not a black "essence" that exists before or outside of the colonial situation; rather, the colonial experience is now a part of black identity. In fact, it has made the process of imagining a new black national identity extremely complex for the emerging countries. The challenging question is how to navigate these troubled waters of identity. The tactics of Brechtian theater served precisely to reveal the complexity of our apparently "natural" situation in the world, hence its appeal for Césaire. The "epic" form and playful, self-conscious theatricality of Césaire's dramatic works are therefore not only a medium for transmitting his message, but an integral part of his representation of the postcolonial condition.

The Tragedy of King Christophe (1963)

Césaire's first drama of decolonization, written between 1959 and 1963, was published in 1963 and first performed at the 1964 Salzburg festival under the direction of Jean-Marie Serreau. *The Tragedy of King Christophe* (*La Tragédie du roi Christophe*) represents a turbulent time in the history of Haiti. The play is set during the civil war that divided the newly independent island nation between a republic in the south governed by the mulattos of the capital Port-au-Prince, and the kingdom of black Haitians in the north ruled by a former cook, Christophe, who upon seizing power assumed the title King Henry I. The play opens with a prologue in which an allegorical cock-fight between birds named "Christophe" and "Pétion" (Pétion headed the republican government in the south) fight to the death, followed by the appearance of a narrator who gives a brief crash-course in Haitian history by explaining the war of independence, Christophe's humble origins, and the recent partition of the country. The first act follows Henry/Christophe's efforts to establish his kingdom. After refusing the offer of the parliament to become the president of Haiti, a position of symbolic importance but very little real power, Christophe declares himself king and decrees that Haiti will have a brilliant, illustrious court, and a hardworking, patriotic peasantry. In a heavily ironic scene foreign aid arrives, not in the form of military or economic assistance, but as a master of ceremonies who

attempts to teach the newly named dukes, earls, and barons courtly manners.
Christophe's coronation names him a king/father/chief, and mixes European
ritual and African rites that invoke the god Shango, with whom Christophe will
be associated throughout the play (Bradby 147). Conscious of pressures both
internal and international that threaten his fledgling kingdom, brought to the
fore by his wife's distinctly Shakespearean prophetic dream, he imagines a gesture of both symbolic and military significance for laying the foundation of his
kingdom: he will build the great citadel of Cap Haitien, which very concretely
brings together a new national identity, a new monarchy, and a new national
work ethic: "Not a palace. Not a castle to protect my well-being. I say a Citadel,
the liberty of all our people. Built by all our people, men and women, young and
old, built by all our people" (Act I, sc. 7). The act ends with the hallucinated
citadel appearing in the night, floating like Valhalla on the clouds.

The second and third acts follow the intertwined trajectories of both the real-
ization and ultimate destruction of King Henry's dream. The interludes between
the acts, along with other scenes interspersed throughout the play, reveal the
attitudes and lives of the Haitian peasantry for whom independence has changed
little, and who must labor to execute Christophe's ambitious projects. The king
meanwhile increasingly finds himself pulled towards a totalitarian dictatorship
by both external political pressure and his desire to found a new civilization. In
his drive to establish a new kingdom, Christophe sows the seeds of his demise.
Cursory executions, forced labor on the citadel and his new palace, and brutally
coercive social progams—in one scene he arbitrarily matches young men and
women and marries them in the name of public morality—resemble more and
more the Terror of the French Revolution or Nazi Germany than the heady dream
of prosperity and righting of past wrongs found in Christophe's discourse at the
beginning of the play. The citadel comes to signify less a monument to national
pride than a symbol of oppression on par with the infamous Bastille prison in
Paris. Already threatened by new tactics from the republic to the south and
increasing unrest from within his kingdom, he suffers an untimely stroke that
paralyzes him almost completely. A series of mutinies, defeats, and betrayals
follow as his hold on power rapidly crumbles, and after a final soliloquy in
which he invokes his African roots, Christophe commits suicide in his palace.
The play ends with pallbearers carrying a casket that becomes heavier as they
move forward: a symbol of the historical significance that the unresolved contradictions Christophe embodied will have on Haiti's future.

Though it represents the historical events surrounding the rise and fall
of Christophe-Henry, *The Tragedy of King Christophe* does not resemble a
documentary or conventional historical drama. A self-conscious theatricality
repeatedly disrupts the history lesson, and fosters a running, critical commentary
on the actions as they unfold. The stage directions to the first act read: "This

entire act is in a clownlike and parodic style, where the serious and the tragic come suddenly to light like a flash of lightning." A range of dramatic devices offers an ironic and often comic counterpoint to the presentation of the weighty issues that play out in both the psychological drama of the king's mind and the political arena in which he acts. The most apparent of these, the character of the court fool Hugonin, accompanies the king throughout the play, punctuating his words and actions with mockery and frank observations that frequently draw the censure of Christophe. Other deployments of theatricality include the scenes at court, which attain a grotesque buffoonery worthy of Molière, the frequent songs that interrupt the action with pointed observations, and the interlude scenes between the acts in which the people of Haiti express their perspective on the events as they unfold. Though the play is a tragedy, as the title indicates, these staging strategies hold the actions, feelings, and beliefs of the hero up to scrutiny. Unlike the Greek tragedy Artistotle idealized, Césaire's play does not permit the spectator to become fully invested in the action, identifying with the hero or feeling fear and pity for him. *The Tragedy of King Christophe* repeatedly alienates the spectator in the Brechtian sense, holding the spectators at a critical distance that allows them to assess the plight of the hero and to see the contradictions and inconsistencies in his behavior, contradictions to which he himself is often blind.

The Tragedy of King Christophe signifies in many registers and defies simple explanation or interpretation. Though it represents early nineteenth-century Haiti, the setting resonates with clear overtones of the Duvalier dictatorship that had been ruling in Haiti since 1957: for instance, Christophe's Royal Dahomets serve a purpose similar to that of the feared and despised Tontons Macoute guard of the Duvalier regime (Pallister 63). The scope of the play, however, exceeds that of one nation's struggle. On a more general plane, it serves as an allegorical caution to nations around the world emerging from centuries of colonialism, many of which followed a trajectory similar to that of Christophe's Haiti by moving quickly from independence into repressive dictatorships. It also raises questions of Western attitudes towards the former colonies, and the underlying pressures that coerce these countries into compliance with European economic self-interest and cultural ideals. The grotesque and ridiculous manners of Christophe's court suggest that European models of government might not easily be imported to suit the needs of emergent nations. In this same vein, Christophe's forced labor and organization of the peasantry, as well as his nationalization of all resources, evokes Stalinist Russia and warns those who would uncritically hail Marxism as a panacea for the ills of colonization. Césaire leads the spectator to conclude that familiar and traditional forms of governmant and nationhood do not meet the needs of the postcolonial era. The dynamic hybrid of African, Carribean, and European culture, most visible in the voodoo religion and the king/father/chief status of Christophe's role as leader, reveal the new political climate created by the colonial experience. The question of how best to act in the complex historical moment of decolonization remains unanswered. Whether because of a hopelessly fraught political situation or his personal choices and flaws, Christophe could not bring the heterogeneous elements of his country together into a viable national and racial identity.

The end of the play, in a typically Brechtian manner, offers the spectator no clear sense of resolution. The struggle continues, and Christophe's death does not provide closure but marks just one more twist of history that will bear on future attempts to establish a government that does not perpetuate the injustices of colonialism. Yet, for all his faults, short-sightedness, egomania, and even brutality, Christophe nevertheless still manages, at moments, to emerge through the parodics as a tragic hero, a man whose actions grew at least initially from the desire to redeem his people from a long history of oppression and to grant his subjects a new sense of pride and dignity in who they are, both as a race and a nation. He ultimately failed to see that his means would make the idealized end unattainable. What could he have done differently? What would we have done in his place? What might the emergent countries of the early 1960s learn from his story? Césaire's complex play leaves the spectators asking these questions, and furnishes no easy answers.

A Season in the Congo (1966)

Césaire's second drama of decolonization also represents a former colony that wins its independence and a charismatic leader who tries, and fails, to realize his idea of a new nation. However, in place of the allegorical and grandly tragic past of Christophe's Haiti, replete with castles, visions, a coronation, battle-fields, and colorful nineteenth-century costumes, the large cast of *A Season in the Congo* moves through a decidedly more banal array of bars, prisons, board rooms, airplane interiors, and offices. In this play, Césaire depicts a grim and very recent historical moment, especially for the spectator of the 1960s: the power struggle following the Congo's independence from Belgium, and the doomed efforts of Patrice Lumumba to save his country from international meddling, civil war, and military dictatorship. The play opens, as did *The Tragedy of King Christophe*, with a performance of sorts: Lumumba works as a beer salesman, weaving a political message into his sales pitch under the watchful eyes of Belgian police: "Drink! Go ahead, drink! Isn't that the only freedom we have left?" This first scene already suggests the often hidden intersection of interests that bear on Congolese actions: the police are suspicious but do not arrest Lumumba because the Belgian minister of the Congo owns the beer company in question. At the end of this scene, and throughout the play, a sanza player wanders on and off, commenting in song about the action as it unfolds. The rest of the first act exposes the complex and shifting alignment of interests that seem to doom the nation even before it can put in place its first independent government. Mokuto, a thinly veiled pseudonym of the eventual dictator Mobutu Sese Seko, begins his treacherous rise to power by feigning solidarity with Lumumba (now the prime minister), while clearly not sharing his ideals. A chorus of foreign bankers plots how to retain their mining investments in the rich Katanga province and bribe the Katangese leaders to split from the rest of the Congo. When the Belgians intervene militarily to rescue their refugees and Katanga secedes, instigating a virtual civil war, Prime Minister Lumumba breaks with his newly chosen King Kala and seeks aid from Moscow, thereby angering the United States and putting in jeopardy any help Lumumba might hope for from the sympathetic but resolutely neutral United Nations Secretary-General Dag Hammarskjöld. Throughout the act, Lumumba emerges as a determined leader who dares to state his ideals, while the other powers selfishly protect their interests.

In the second act, the rapidly deteriorating situation forces Lumumba into making tough decisions. He closes a local newspaper critical of his regime and arrests its editor. He then agrees to escalate the civil war by calling for an invasion of the Katanga region, unaware that his army will commit atrocities against the Baluba ethnic group. In a frightening and surreal scene, the voice of war rises over an armed mob chanting a euphoric thirst for blood. The international outrage over this massacre further convinces Lumumba that drastic measures are necessary, and in a discourse worthy of Sartre's unapologetic existentialist heroes he vows to pursue without regret his campaign to unify the Congo. In a lyrical scene, he and a dance-hall girl poetically imagine the good that will come out of the current violence and chaos. The poetic dance is brusquely followed by King Kala's angry tirade, and in the following scene Lumumba tries to calm the fears of his wife who rightfully believes that his closest allies, Kala and Mokutu, are plotting his downfall. A radio broadcast confirms this, and Lumumba vows to fight the King. He seeks to rouse the people with a stirring broadcast of his own, but a Ghanaian United Nations peacekeeping force denies him access to the airwaves in the name of neutrality—a neutrality that ties Lumumba's hands and plays into those of his enemies. Mokutu's storm-troopers invade Lumumba's villa and arrest him, but not before he laments the sad state not only of the Congo, and of all its neighbors who bear the yoke of colonial rule; Lumumba wishes for a "Pan-African" front against all oppression while the short-sighted Mokutu thinks only of the Congo (Pallister 77).

The third act portrays Lumumba's escape from prison, managed through an appeal to his jailors' mistrust of Mokutu, and his attempt to reclaim power with a coup. He assumes a nearly Christ-like quality: betrayed by a treacherous ally, he comes bearing the "good news" of African pride, thus echoing Césaire's *Notebook of a Return to My Native Land* (Pallister 79). To his wife Pauline's distress, he expresses his willingness to be sacrificed for his country. Mokutu and Kala burst in with an armed guard and offer him a lesser position in their government, which he refuses. Lumumba is arrested, and in a political deal Mokutu hands him over to the Katangese, who despise him. After a scene in New York where Dag Hammarskjöld despairingly recognizes that Lumumba's life is in danger and that some of the blood for his imminent death is on the hands of the United Nations, the Katangese brutally beat and execute Lumumba on stage. In the final scenes, Hammarskjöld, a banker, Tzumbi (the Katangese leader), Kala, and Mokutu file across the stage one by one, disculpating themselves of Lumumba's death. Mokutu seizes power, and in a scene that Césaire added to the final version of the play he addresses a crowd in Kinshasa to name a boulevard after Lumumba and raise a statue to him, thereby attempting to co-opt the popularity of the fallen leader. Just before the curtain, he orders the massacre of the crowd and exits, leaving the audience with the image of a stage littered with fallen bodies.

A *Season in the Congo* explores the havoc left in the wake of colonialism on a global level, and is a more overtly political play than *The Tragedy of King Christophe*. The internal psychodrama of Christophe is replaced by an intricate web of external pressures and interests that determine the characters' behavior. This change of focus entails different staging strategies. Césaire once again deploys a broad range of Brechtian alienation effects that offer the spectator multiple perspectives on the action, but does so in a more focused manner than in *The Tragedy of King Christophe*. The sanza player fills a role similar to that of Christophe's fool Hugonin, though with significant differences: he remains generally disengaged from the events as they unfold, often singing his songs between the scenes. His commentary therefore springs more from the position of a spectator watching the action and less from that of a character actively participating in represented events. Césaire also reserves the parody that he prescribed for the entire first act of *The Tragedy of King Christophe* to target a single group, the caricatured international bankers who sport top hats and cigars and speak grotesquely in verse. Other alienation effects include panels with writing and maps lowered from above that announce and illustrate what is happening on the stage, the voices of "Revindication" and "War" which raise themselves over the action to incite the mobs to violence, and the many moments where characters break into song. All of these staging techniques disrupt the linear or "realistic" progression of the plot, and lead the spectators to grasp the complicated web of interests and points of view that shape the troubled history of Congolese independence as it unfolds. The Brechtian staging does not allow them to accept the plight of Lumumba and the Congo as an inevitable or somehow "natural" course of events.

Although they both draw inspiration from Brecht, *A Season in the Congo* and *The Tragedy of King Christophe* portray the main character in a very different manner. The similarities between Lumumba's story and that of Christophe are of course numerous: both quickly rise to power and ultimately fail to realize their dream of an independent nation, of a *black* nation that fosters and guarantees the pride emblematized in Césaire's notion of negritude. However, in *The Tragedy of King Christophe*, the alienation effects offered a pointed commentary not only on the political situation but also on Christophe himself. Christophe had his own vision, as symbolized in the hallucinated citadel: his increasingly brutal regime resulted as much from the political situation as from his driving ambition to realize a very personal ideal and dream, one that was as much the glory of Christophe as it was of his nation and his race. Lumumba, on the other hand, eschews personal glory and rejects the kingship, even when it is offered to him. Futhermore, unlike Christophe he never loses touch with the plight of the common people; he repeatedly seeks them out, relates to them, and remains their champion even after his death. The internal dialectic that characterizes Christophe, whose drive to build a country also leads to its (and his) downfall, is absent in Lumumba. His recourse to war and oppression does not serve a personal vision, but results from the external pressures that threaten the very existence of an independent Congolese state. Lumumba remains generally above reproach and blame for the gruesome and tragic events, even those in which he participates. It is worth noting that the sanza player's comments are poetic and cryptic and, unlike Hugonin's disrespectful mockery of Christophe and his policies, comment on and lament the general situation more than the actions of Lumumba himself. As David Bradby points out, Lumumba is not truly a "tragic" hero, for he bears no tragic flaw other than his own admirable principles (150). Lumumba, unlike Christophe, never loses the moral high ground. If there is a tragic figure in this play it would be Hammarskjöld, who in the end sadly realizes that his well-intentioned policy of neutrality served Lumumba's enemies and brought about his death.

Addressing many of the same issues as *The Tragedy of King Christophe, A Season in the Congo* more clearly emphasizes how decolonization is not merely a question of the isolated, internal problems of an emerging independent state and its leaders. The whole world is implicated, and if the responsibility lies on the shoulders of the Congolese, it also falls on cold-war politics, multinational capitalism, and racism on a global level. In the name of anti-communism, "humanitarian" military maneuvers, and even "peace-keeping" neutrality, the actions of Belgium, the United States, and the United Nations incite the civil war and influence its outcome, contributing to Lumumba's downfall and the rise of a dictatorship in the Congo. Furthermore, the lack of solidarity among African peoples, most notably in the Katangese secession, betrays a policy of preserving parochial interests that plays into the hands of the former colonial powers. Out of this fraught situation where, in a typically Brechtian manner, good engenders evil (Hammarskjöld) and evil is done in the name of righteousness (Lumumba's invasion of Katanga), Lumumba emerges as the voice of disinterested reason, a prophet and martyr who alone understood that individual identity, whether that of a person, a people, or a race, is always situated in and shaped by a greater historical situation. However, he too could not transcend the troubled situation in which he was thrown. Had he succeeded, he would have not only nominally but substantively ended colonial rule over his country.

A Tempest (1968)

Unlike its predecessors, Césaire's third play does not represent factual people, places, and events. *A Tempest* (*Une Tempête*), an adaptation of Shakespeare's *The Tempest*, transforms this familiar canonical work into a parable of race relations. Productions of *The Tempest* have often dwelt on its colonial overtones, but *A Tempest* explicitly sets the action in terms of the struggle between a colonizing European master and the colonized indigenous slaves. Césaire tinkers with Shakespeare's text, adding to the list of characters a few brief but significant specifications. Prospero's slaves, the monster-like Caliban and the sprite Ariel, are both of color in *A Tempest*: Caliban is black and Ariel is mulatto. In another significant deviation, the master/slave dynamic dominates Césaire's play at the expense of both the love story between Ferdinand and Miranda and the political intrigue among the Europeans that compete with it in Shakespeare's text. Césaire also adds an additional deity, the Yoruba trickster god Eshu, to those who bless the marriage of the young couple. In its representation of racial identity, the play further strays from the Shakespearian text when it prescribes cross-race casting through the use of masks. In a brief prologue to the play, a Master of Ceremonies distributes these to the attendant cast in a seemingly arbitrary manner. Césaire specifies that he wrote the play for a *théâtre nègre*, an all-black company; since Caliban, Ariel, and Eshu are the only characters of color, adherence to Césaire's indications would mean that the white Europeans, the majority of the roles, would be played by black actors in white masks.

After this prologue, the play opens very much like Shakespeare's, showing the shipwreck of King Alonso and his entourage in a storm brewed by Prospero's magical powers. Prospero, the deposed Duke of Milan, seizes the chance to avenge his years of exile. His daughter Miranda feels pity for the shipwrecked sailors, and Prospero explains the treacherous past that led him and his daughter to be banished on this island. Ariel, a spirit of the air and Prospero's mulatto servant, arrives to announce that he has done his master's will and asks to be set free, a request Prospero angrily defers. Prospero then calls in Caliban, his black servant, who enters with a defiant "Uhuru!" and a bitter battle of wills ensues. In a pointed commentary on racial inequality, Caliban remarks that Prospero's "magic" powers are nothing more than the education, knowledge, and technology that he keeps for himself. Prospero retorts with a barrage of racial insults. Caliban announces that he has chosen a new name, or rather, no name at all: "Call me X," he says, for his true name has been forgotten with the language he spoke before the arrival of Prospero. Prospero summons Ariel and decides to spare the Europeans, his kinsmen, and directs his anger towards the recalcitrant Caliban. Ariel, who pitied the Europeans, joyfully agrees, and with his powers brings the young prince Ferdinand (Alonso's son) and Miranda together. At the end of the first act, Prospero provisionally enslaves Ferdinand as his servant.

The second act opens with a tense confrontation between Ariel and Caliban. Ariel warns his fellow slave of Prospero's clearly superior power, and tries to convince him that peaceful persuasion tactics will succeed much sooner than any sort of violent confrontation. Caliban mocks Ariel's belief that Prospero's brutal exterior hides a well of goodness that they need only tap to achieve their freedom. The two part amiably, however, wishing each other the best of luck in their respective tactics. The remainder of the act returns more or less faithfully to the political intrigue among the shipwrecked Europeans in Shakespeare's text. Distraught and bereaved by the apparent loss of his son, the King repents of his evil past. Prospero taunts them, via the powers of Ariel, with a magical banquet that disappears before their eyes. When they finally partake of the food, they fall asleep, leaving themselves open to the murderous plots of two of the European noblemen, the ambitious Antonio and Sebastien. Ariel intervenes, however, and spares the repentant king: a sign of Prospero's mercy towards his own countrymen that sharply contrasts with his cruelty towards his two non-Eurpoean servants.

In the final act, Caliban meets up with two of the shipwrecked sailors, the drunken Trinculo and Stephano, and the three plot the takeover of the island and the thrones of Milan and Naples. In another deviation from Shakespeare, who called for a ridiculously ingenuous Caliban worshipping and serving the drunkards, Césaire's Trinculo and Stephano quickly become the footsoldiers of a wily and determined Caliban who knows exactly what he is up against. In the meantime, Prospero has prepared the wedding of Ferdinand and Miranda and summons the goddesses of ancient Greece to bestow their blessings on the couple. An uninvited guest, Eshu, disrupts the solemn ceremony, frightens the goddesses away, and performs a provocative dance in which beats the wedding party with his phallus. Prospero's magic powers fail against this non-European intruder, and his powerlessness, or *impotence*, contrasts with the phallic

mischief of Eshu. Furious over the spoiled wedding feast, he blames Caliban
for his troubles and vows revenge. Caliban meanwhile mobilizes his drunken
"troops," explaining that the magic that weighs them down is really Prospero's
tear-gas. They are apprehended and imprisoned. Prospero decides to return to
Europe, sets Ariel free, and pardons Trinculo and Stephano, as well as all the
other Europeans who years earlier had plotted against him. Caliban will not
grovel for forgiveness, however, and issues a defiant condemnation of Prospero
and his brutal reign over the island. In a last deviation from Shakespeare, Prospero changes his mind and chooses to remain on the island while all the others
return to Europe. The final scene, presumably several years later, shows him
alone and miserable, for Caliban has disappeared into the forest. In a paranoid
fit, he shoots his gun into the air, screaming that he will "defend civilization,"
but there is no answer other than the "shreds of Caliban's song" in the distance
as the curtain falls.

It is not difficult to interpret *A Tempest* as a playful parable of the colonial
situation. To read the humor, masks, and magic of *A Tempest* as merely a "light"
reprise of the same issues addressed in Césaire's previous two plays, however,
would be to overlook the sophisticated comment the play issues on racial identity.
Where the god Shango cast its shadow over the hero and events of *The Tragedy
of King Christophe*, the trickster Eshu more closely emblematizes *A Tempest*.
As Eshu disrupted the wedding feast, so Césaire intervenes in Shakespeare's
text to disrupt the assumptions that underlie the Western canon. His playful
staging strategies offer a radical critique of identities that were taking shape in
Shakepeare's time: the civilized "colonizer" and the savage "colonized," which
often double the racial categories of "white" and "colored."

The elaborate play of masks Césaire prescribes in the prologue constitutes
the play's most prominent subversive staging strategy and, far more than a
gimmick, participates integrally in the message Césaire brings to the spectator.
Throughout the play, the masks alienate the identity of the characters, particularly
where race is concerned. In the case of the European characters, for example,
the black performers remain visible under the masks of whiteness, suggesting
that race is more a performance than a biological or essential identity, something
one *does* rather than what one *is*. The masks of blackness worn by Caliban and
Ariel, however, are no less "false." Caliban's angry final tirade explicitly links
this staging practice to the colonial ideology of race:

> Prospero, you are a great illusionist: deception knows you well. And you have lied to
> me so much, lied about the world, about myself, that you finally imposed an image
> on me, an image of myself, an "underdeveloped" you say, an "underachiever," that
> is how you have made me see myself, and I hate this image! It is false! (88, my
> translation)

The masks emblematize the repressive racial identity which Caliban himself has internalized, and in which he has misrecognized himself as an inferior. Césaire's very literal masks here evoke the figurative ones that Frantz Fanon describes in his well-known analysis of racial identity under colonialism *Peau noire, masques blancs* (*Black Skin, White Masks*, 1956). In his final defiant speech, Caliban denounces this image's apparently natural and essential grounding to reveal, to himself, to other characters, and to the spectators the history of power relations that generated and perpetuated it to his detriment.

The use of masks exemplifies a Brechtian alienation effect. In *A Tempest*, the masks reveal race as a historical construction, and alienate the characters' assumption that the status quo of race relations on the island is somehow "natural." It also betrays the figurative ideological "masks" of identity that Prospero propogates in the dehumanizing discourse he sytematically directs at Caliban, revealing it as a rhetoric of power and oppression whose claim to "naturalness" is enforced only by the technological superiority that he so jealously guards. Prospero's meteorological machinations, most notably the storm after which the play is titled, further unveil the human mediation behind an apparently "natural" state of affairs. Significantly, although Caliban in the end rejects the mask of identity that the play so evidently imposes upon him in the prologue, Césaire denies his audience the sight of this liberating gesture. In contrast to the very visible imposition of the masks onto already racialized bodies in the prologue, the symmetrical unmasking of the end takes place invisibly in the wings. Caliban's renouncement of racial identity is therefore double: he refuses to play the racialized role both of the character who is no longer willing to be Prospero's "savage" slave, and also of the racially specific black performer who assumed this role in the prologue. The play leaves the spectator no image of the liberated subject who transcends or otherwise escapes from a racializing and racist discursive regime. At the play's end the spectator is stuck with the familiar racial identities of the white masked "Prospero" and the black actor performing him, the emblem of an exhausted white/black racial binary. Caliban might have escaped this dynamic, but Prospero (and the actor playing him) does not, nor ultimately do the spectators for whom the liberated subject remains an unimagined, unrealized dream.

In addition to its more complex staging of racial identity, *A Tempest* also differs from its predecessors by broadening the range of its commentary. Christophe's Haiti and the Congo of 1961 can be read as metaphors for the emerging nations, but they do not address racial identity outside of the context of decolonization. It may be true that *A Season in the Congo* suggests that negritude knows no national boundaries, as expressed in Lumumba's call for a Pan-African sense of solidarity and brotherhood, but in all the countries mentioned the racial injustices resulted from colonial rule. *A Tempest* extends its comment to the black populations of the colonizing powers themselves, most explicitly to the United States. Césaire wrote this play during the height of the civil rights movement, and from Martinique he followed closely the events that were taking place in his "backyard" in the Western hemisphere. Caliban's belligerent and uncompromising discourse clearly evokes that of Malcolm X, quite explicitly in the "Call me X" scene, and Ariel incarnates the non-violence advocated by Martin Luther King. Their disagreement on how to proceed against racist regimes resounds with pertinence for black populations worldwide: Ariel earns his freedom, but at a cost, and his belief in Prospero's "goodness" seems naive in light of the former master's brutality and overt racism toward Caliban in the final scene. As for Caliban, though he might more realistically assess the conscience of Prospero, his status at the end of the play remains to be defined. Césaire ultimately leaves the spectator to ponder the complexities of the historical situation and to weigh the benefits of different courses of action. He advocates neither position—both Ariel and Caliban meet with a measure of success in their struggle. Nor does he suggest the struggle has ended; as in his previous plays, Césaire shows the negotiation of a historical situation at a critical moment, and through an astute manipulation of theatricality brings to light the unresolved contradictions that propel history forward throughout the play, and continue to do so after its final curtain.

REFERENCES

Bradby, David. *Modern French Drama 1940–1990.* 2nd ed. New York: Cambridge UP, 1991.

Césaire, Aimé. *Une Saison au Congo.* Paris: Seuil, 1973.

——. *Une Tempête.* Paris: Seuil, 1969.

——. *La Tragédie du roi Christophe.* Paris: Présence Africaine, 1963.

Fanon, Frantz. *Peau noire, masques blancs.* Paris: Seuil, 1952.

Livingston, Robert Eric. "Decolonizing Theatre: Césaire, Serreau and the Drama of Négritude." *Imperialism and Theatre: Essays on World Theatre, Drama and Performance.* Ed. J. Ellen Gainor. New York: Routledge, 1995.

Pallister, Janis L. *Aimé Césaire.* New York: Twayne, 1991.

Toumson, Roger, and Simonne Henry-Valmore. *Aimé Césaire: le nègre inconsolé.* Paris: Syros, 1993.

"Un poète politique: Aimé Césaire." Interview. *Magazine Littéraire* 34 (Nov. 1969): 27–32.

DISCUSSION QUESTIONS

1. Why did Césiaire choose the theater (instead of the novel, for example) to represent the postcolonial situation?

2. Taking into account the many stage indications Césaire provides, put yourself in the position of director/designer and imagine your own production of one of his plays. What would the stage look like? The costumes? What special lighting, props, or set pieces are necessary? Justify your production choices by explaining how they help convey Césaire's political message.

3   Césaire's theater shows how the complexity of the postcolonial world shapes events both past and present. What vision does it offer of the future? Does Césaire leave the spectator with a message, a call to action, or a political agenda? What "lessons" do we as spectators learn from his plays?

4. Césaire's *negritude* refuses the idea of a biological, essential, or "natural" racial identity. Instead he proposes a historical account of racial identity. How do his plays suggest the historical—and therefore changeable—status of what it means to be "black" or "white"?

CHAPTER SEVEN

South America's "Guyane": Model of Francophone Diversity

Marcia G. Parker and Beverley G. David

A francophone "island" in South America where its peoples form a rich composite of languages, cultural backgrounds, and histories, French Guiana (la Guyane) is a department of France, along with her Caribbean sisters Martinique and Guadeloupe.[1] Its early history of colonization by Portugal, Holland, England, and France, and significant links to Africa primarily through the slave trade, are reflected in its languages, family traditions, foods, celebrations, and music. Although political association with France is about to enter its fourth century, Guiana maintains a distinct and separate identity. Many people are unaware of this French presence in South America.

Guiana is a rich country in terms of its natural resources — human, mineral, marine, forest, water — situated on a sparsely populated extensive land mass. Its ethnic base includes the indigenous Amerindians, the Alukus (various communities descended from fugitive slaves), and the Creoles all of whom form a heterogeneous society with unique histories and customs. The population of Guiana has doubled within the last thirty years primarily through immigration and/or "implantation" of diverse groups from the Caribbean, other South American neighbors, and Asia. Although these new residents are not fully integrated into the society at large, with a positive political will Guiana has the potential to be strong and cohesive.

Geography

Geographically, Guiana is situated on the northern coast of South America between 3° and 6° north latitude and between 52° and 56° west longitude, and shares a continuous geological shield (called the Guiana plateau) with Surinam and Guyana.[2] She is the smallest of the three located on the Guiana plateau (Mouren-Lascaux 14–15). From her more open areas along the coast to her almost impenetrable forests, from her swamps and lowlands to her mountainous terrain, Guiana's geography reflects another form of diversity.

Natural boundaries include the northern coast, formed entirely by the Atlantic Ocean, the 500 km [313 mi] border with Surinam formed by the Maroni

River to the west, the 600 km [375 mi] border with Brazil formed by the Oyapock River to the east and the Tumuc-Humac Mountains to the south (Rivière 7). Many rivers reach into the interior, but challenge travelers seeking to navigate the waterways because of numerous rapids (rocky barriers called "sauts") along their course. A trip up or down one of these rivers can take several days. Such rugged terrain might have discouraged peace among the different ethnic groups. However, greater outside threats such as slave trade in the past and present day pressures from metropolitan France (for example, importing ethnic groups) provide incentives for these communities to work together.

This part of France is situated 1,500 km [938 mi] from Martinique and 7,100 km [4,438 mi] from France. The largest of France's departments, Guiana covers a total surface area of 91,000 km² [35,547 mi²], approximately one sixth the size of France. Primary tropical forests cover 90% of this area, with its highest point, Mont Tabulaire, rising to a peak of approximately 800 m [2,640 ft]. Apart from three small islands off its Atlantic coast called "les îles du Salut," former home of the penal colony until 1947, Guiana is continental (Mouren-Lascaux 15).

The equatorial climate is tempered by the dense forest cover and the effect of trade winds. Temperatures range between approximately 32°C [90°F] during the day and 22°C [72°F] at night with humidity reaching 90%. Annual rainfall can vary between 3200 mm [142 in] at Kaw and 2000 mm [79 in] at Saint Laurent. Two rainy (December–February, April-July) and two dry seasons (March-April, August-December) divide the year (Sanité 2).

Because of its geographical location and geological background, Guiana does not suffer from natural disasters such as earthquakes and hurricanes that plague some of the islands of the Caribbean region. The fortunate combination of abundant rainfall, high temperatures, and year-round sunshine results in the lush tropical vegetation that covers most of the country, especially striking when seen from the air.

Census figures from the 1990s suggest a population of approximately 136,000 (Bordry 7). However, it is very difficult to provide accurate population figures because of unusual patterns of migration. The influx of refugees from Surinam and illegal immigration from Brazil necessitate viewing census figures as estimations. Although the total population seems relatively small, the recent demographic explosion appears remarkable when compared to 65,000 inhabitants of twenty years ago. France's "Green Plan" to implant 30,000 new citizens did contribute significantly to the rapid increase in the population (Delannon, "Réalité").

Most of the population (95%) is concentrated on a coastal strip 300 km [185 mi] long and 20 km [12.5 mi] wide along the Atlantic Ocean. This densely populated band constitutes a mere 6% of the total surface area and contains the largest cities. This may be explained in part by the fact that a major portion of the economic base is located here: fishing along the coast and in the rivers, agricultural development on this lowland area, the space station, import/export activities from the ports and the airport.

The capital city, Cayenne, lies on the Atlantic coast. Alone, it accounts for almost two-thirds of the population (1990 census, 41,637 or 70,000 including suburbs) (France, French Embassy 10). Cayenne serves as the administrative center as well as the main port of entry into Guiana. A very diverse capital, most ethnic groups that comprise Guiana choose to live here. There is a distinct flavor to Cayenne in terms of ambiance. The houses are painted bright colors (red, yellow, pink, green), are often two stories with a balcony, and have shutters for the windows. Many windows take advantage of the cool Atlantic breezes that reduce the impact of the hot, humid tropical conditions (Mouren-Lascaux 85).

Kourou (13,963), a city on the coast west of Cayenne going toward the border with Surinam, is the site of the space station established in 1964. The French National Center for Space Studies (CNES) chose this site which is approximately 9 miles long from among 14 other possibilities around the world. Several factors supported this decision: the relatively small population, proximity to the equator facilitating launching due to a weaker gravitational pull, direction of launch toward the ocean useful in the event of accidents. The space station attracts more than 6,000 visitors per year (Mouren-Lascaux 125–126).

Saint Laurent du Maroni (14,061), the city closest to the border with Surinam, is the geopolitical boundary between these two countries (France, French Embassy 10). However, common historical and cultural bonds encourage very close informal relations between the peoples of these border regions. They tend to speak the same languages or versions of the same languages. They also share similar activities in terms of mechanisms for survival put into place over centuries.

History

The geographical location of the Guiana plateau, its tropical climate and promise of riches brought European adventurers and conquerors to the shores of French Guiana early in the seventeenth century. Portugal and Spain had previously claimed and divided South America in a treaty (1494), but the immense size prevented them from discouraging other countries, particularly France, England, and Holland, from claiming pieces for themselves. However, difficult living conditions combined with resistance of indigenous populations and conflict between competing European nations impeded extensive colonization (Mouren-Lascaux 19–20).

Discovery of a primitive ax in 1988 led researchers to believe Amerindian or pre-Amerindian people inhabited this land since 10,000 B.C. (Mouren-Lascaux 18). Europeans encountered native peoples of several semi-nomadic tribes living as hunters and gatherers. In 1499 an estimated 30,000 Amerindians lived on the Guiana plateau, but European encroachment pushed many into the interior. The number of Amerindians decreased substantially through war, but even more so from European diseases. Today, six groups remain: the oldest being the Arawaks, about 150 people in Guiana and 3000 more in the neighboring country of Surinam, the Palikours, about 400, and 800 in Brazil, the Wayanas, about 1000 including those in Surinam and Brazil, the Galibis, about 2000, and two ethnic sub-groups of the Tupi-Guarani, the Wayapis or Oyampis, about 500, and the Emerillons, about 150 (Mouren-Lascaux 40–46).

Some descendants of these ethnic groups lived in contact with the succeeding groups of immigrants who settled in Guiana, but others have chosen to live apart. The French government established a protected zone in the interior in 1977 to which access is denied without official authorization, supposedly to allow indigenous groups to maintain their cultures. Not all Guianese agree with this ruling, nor with its expressed intent (Mouren-Lascaux 50–53).

French influence in Guiana began with Daniel de La Touche de La Ravardière's expedition in 1604, but did not succeed on a long term basis until 1676 with the governorship of M. de Lézy. During those seventy-two years, control fluctuated between Holland and France, with a brief takeover by England. An expedition to colonize this land brought the first West African slaves in 1652. For the next two hundred years, France continued to send colonists, including missionaries and slaves, in an attempt to settle the region. Many died from malaria, initiating this area's reputation as being inhospitable, a reputation later reinforced by the establishment of a penal colony. The most notorious expedition, supported by Louis XV and directed by Choiseul, arrived with 16,000 European settlers, 10,000 of whom died from tropical diseases. Some survived by escaping to three little islands off the coast, then renamed for the safety they provided, les îles du Salut, or "Salvation Islands" (Mouren-Lascaux 23–27).

During two centuries of slavery (1652–1848), large numbers of slaves escaped, forming groups known as maroons or "marrons," the word for fugitive slaves. They established communities deep in the Amazon forest, returning to many African cultural practices and adopting survival methods similar to the Amerindians: hunting and gathering. They also conducted frequent raids on plantations, freeing more slaves, and organized significant rebellions in 1700, 1710, 1740, 1770 and 1796 (Guyane, OCCE). After unsuccessful attempts to pursue and destroy the maroons, neighboring Dutch authorities offered peace treaties in 1760 and 1767 to several of the larger groups, the Djukas, Saramacas, and Matawais. These societies gained official acknowledgment of their freedom and the right to stay on the territory they inhabited by agreeing to stop pillaging and to return future escapees. New fugitive slaves after that time had to form independent communities which became the Bonis, Paramacas, and Kwintis. Those who did not escape often performed other acts of resistance including abortion, self-poisoning, poisoning of the livestock, and covert help to the maroons, at great risk of torture or death (Guyane, OCCE).

The Revolution of 1789 in France freed the slaves and brought a new group of "immigrants"—deportees who were victims of changing governments and laws. Many were priests who remained loyal to the church, refusing to pledge their allegiance to the government. Left to their own survival, numerous exiles died because they were ill prepared to adjust to such a different environment. Once more history contributed to the disrepute of this land (Mouren-Lascaux 27–28).

Rapidly changing events in Europe between 1789 and 1815 affected the lives of those living in Guiana. Napoleon reactivated the sugar cane industry by reestablishing slavery. However, wars in Europe encouraged the Portuguese to take over Guiana, only to lose it once again through the treaty of Paris in 1814. At that time there were approximately 2,700 free inhabitants and 13,000 slaves in addition to the Amerindians. Slavery was finally abolished in 1848 by the Congress of Vienna, giving the French government headed by Napoleon III cause to establish a penal colony there to supply the needed labor force. The original plan expected these prisoners to settle the colony after their terms expired. However, France began to send its worst criminals who would not be good candidates for farming, even if they survived the terrible conditions and treatment in the jails and labor camps. Stories filtering back to France reinforced the reputation of a "green hell." 70,000 prisoners from France, Algeria, and other French colonies were shipped to the penal colony between 1852 and 1939 (Mouren-Lascaux 28–31).

Because of this immediate continuation of another "slavery" that included a majority of white men, a hypothesis related to the psychological effect on newly-freed blacks purports a different attitude toward their own former enslavement from those freed in other countries. Seeing white men in shackles performing the work of slaves for almost one hundred years (until 1947) diminished the strong connection between race and oppression. In turn, the role of race decreased as a discriminating factor. Oppression under these conditions could be viewed more in terms of power and profit than in terms of ethnic origin (Delannon, "Réalité").

Earlier myths of a land of gold were reinforced in 1854 with the discovery of a significant quantity of gold, bringing another group of immigrants to Guiana—prospectors. The hostility of the climate and geography once again prevented many from "striking it rich." Gold fever never died; prospectors and adventurers continued their searches with another large wave in 1901. Even today gold remains an attractive force (Mouren-Lascaux 31–32).

Although World War I and World War II did not bring military conflict directly to Guiana, they did influence its history. At the outbreak of World War I the French government summoned young men from Guiana who had never visited France to fight and die for its cause. During the period between the wars, efforts to begin closing the penal colony were successful and no more prisoners were sent after 1939. Because World War II began, prisoners remained until the penal colony was finally closed in 1947. During the Second World War, Guiana initially supported the Vichy government, but switched its allegiance to Free France. The United States then built an airstrip just outside Cayenne to be used for defense purposes (Mouren-Lascaux 33–35).

Soon after the war, France changed the status of Guiana, Martinique, Guadeloupe, and Réunion (an island in the Indian Ocean) to that of overseas departments (DOM, départements d'outre-mer), thus technically awarding them the same rights as departments in metropolitan France. French Guiana officially became a part of France, its inhabitants becoming French citizens. French citizenship entitled them to vote, to elect representatives to the National Assembly and Senate, and to hold office (Delannon, "Réalité").

With the war in Algeria and its subsequent independence in 1962, France needed to find a new location for its space center. Realizing that Guiana provided an ideal location, France installed its rocket launching facilities in the area of Kourou in 1964 (Guyane, OCCE). Although people have not dissociated Guiana from its history as a dumping ground for convicts and others exiled from France, that history is fading and even becoming somewhat romanticized with the passage of time. The space center is replacing the penal colony as the identifying element of Guiana. The center has significantly influenced economic development; nevertheless, Guianese leaders understand the importance of encouraging growth of diverse industries to bolster the economy and self-reliance of its citizens.

This cursory review of Guiana's history is intended to help one understand why these citizens represent a great variety of ethnic groups and how this part of France can provide a model of many groups of people coming together from different backgrounds, for divergent reasons, unified in part by common political goals. The first inhabitants, Amerindians, make up only 3.3% of the population. The population count in 1993 of the different groups includes 49,000 Creoles, 30,000 Haitians, 10,000 Europeans, 10,000 Brazilians, 6,000 Boschs, Boni and Saramacas, 5,730 Amerindians, 1,500 Hmong and 1,200 Guyanese (from Guyana, formerly British Guiana) (France, French Embassy 9). Once again, the figures have to be seen as estimates, because it is virtually impossible to monitor border traffic between Guiana, Surinam, and Brazil.

The largest group, Creoles, could be called the backbone of Guiana both because of their strength in numbers and political activism and because of their heritage. Their mixture is much more intricate than a simple combination of European and African or Amerindian, etc. They are truly an amalgam of Africans (both former slaves and free workers from Senegal), Brazilians, Hindus, Chinese and Europeans. Other than the Amerindians, these people are descendants of the first settlers of French Guiana (Mouren-Lascaux 60–62). Forming the largest group of inhabitants and being of mixed heritage, the Creoles may offer another reason for a greater propensity to accept differences between the ethnic groups composing Guiana's population. This group representing the very epitome of diversity coming together offers a political strength proposing cooperation among all groups from different backgrounds.

During the post-slavery period, the French government solicited Chinese and Hindus to bolster the labor force. They now work mainly in commerce. Since Guiana became a department, many Brazilians, Haitians and Surinamese came to find jobs, providing a cheaper labor force for France's projects. Employment was first found in the forest industries and in construction, especially with the building of the space center in Kourou in 1964. The Hmong community arrived in a more controversial atmosphere when the French government decided to send the boat people en masse to French Guiana in 1979 rather than integrate them into metropolitan France. With each succeeding wave of immigrants, the demography of Guiana's population changes significantly (Mouren-Lascaux 63–66).

Government and Politics

As a colony of France, the only political power originally rested with the appointed governor or prefect until 1878, when the colonial General Council came into existence. From that date on Guiana was represented in the French Parliament as a colony. Full representation and voting privileges did not exist until the status of department was mandated in 1946. Guianese voters elect two representatives to the National Assembly and one senator to the Senate, both housed in Paris. The President of France still appoints a prefect to represent the national government and to supervise local authorities. As in all French departments, the General Council determines the departmental budget and oversees education, utilities, and social welfare. Administrative divisions include two districts (arrondissements), 19 counties (cantons) and 22 townships (communes). Voters elect the 19 members of the General Council, the members of each municipal council, and the 31 members of the Regional Council. The regional system came into being in France in 1972, but the government did not designate Guiana as a region until 1982 (France, French Embassy 5).

Groups rallying for independence from France became quite popular in the

1970s, encouraged by Guyana's independence from Great Britain in 1966 and Surinam's independence from the Netherlands in 1975. Two of the best known are MOGUYDE (Mouvement Guyanais pour la Décolonisation) and FNLG (Front National de Libération de la Guyane). France imprisoned some of its more vocal leaders in an attempt to discourage their progress (Taubira-Delannon 84–85). Possibilities for autonomy looked bright for those involved until the Socialist political victory in France. With the election of François Mitterrand from the Socialist Party came a deflation of the ranks wanting independence in Guiana. Many felt their needs could be addressed through governmental channels opened by a leftist government. Separatist tendencies were further diffused in 1982 by the decentralization movement in France. More authority would be delegated to local governments (Delannon, "Réalité").

Various political parties presented candidates for the legislative elections of 1993, some of them extensions of parties found in metropolitan France and some unique to Guiana. Such a heterogeneous population would logically support a variety of parties and candidates promoting disparate platforms. These parties include the Front National (FN), Rassemblement pour la République - Union pour la Démocratie Française (RPR-UDF), Walwari, Génération Ecologie, MDES (Mouvement de Décolonisation et d'Emancipation Sociale), Parti Socialiste Guyanais (PSG), and PNPG (Parti Nationaliste Progressiste Guyanais). In an effort to solidify support for his economic policies in France, President Jacques Chirac called for early legislative elections in the spring of 1997. Chirac lost his majority, but Guianese incumbents Léon Bertrand (RPR) and Christiane Taubira-Delannon (Walwari) won reelection to the National Assembly for a new five-year term (Delannon, "Réalité").

The Walwari party represents a dramatic change in the political scene in Guiana. A new political party as of 1992 [the title comes from a Galibi word meaning fan, "éventail" in French, to represent leadership offering a breath of new life, a fanning of the flames or reenergizing], Walwari upset the long-standing power structure of the Guianese socialist party. Christiane Taubira-Delannon and people like her who had been involved in political movements for autonomy in the 70s believed the dominating PSG was vulnerable due to inaction and abuse of power. She reiterated during her campaign that her party was not seeking independence from France, but "democracy and development" in order to continue her battle against poverty, unemployment, poor living conditions, and exclusion. She emphasized the importance of dignity for the people of French Guiana (Delannon, *Conquérir* 89).

Results of her first four years were the creation of the public land institution, mining reform, social and fiscal dispensations granted to enterprises and the agricultural sector for the creation of jobs, and grants awarded to communities. She arranged visits for young students to organizations with scientific, technical, and ecological missions, took students to Europe for exchanges with youths of other nationalities and lectured often in schools. Taubira-Delannon, an economist, understood the importance of introducing young people to a variety of careers and possibilities by broadening their school experiences (Delannon, "Réalité"). Citizens of Guiana as well as interested outside observers are watching closely to ascertain if a progressive movement takes hold providing a more financially independent department or if the more established political powers continue to dominate. Control of other political offices by reformist governmental leaders and improvement of the economy will determine the success of this or any other new political party in Guiana.

Economy

In all of France, the economy during the 1990s experienced serious problems of unemployment, at times between 10 and 14% in metropolitan France and 30% in Guiana. Other overseas departments suffered an even greater rate of joblessness. 1988 salaries averaged 35,000 francs (about $7,000) in Guiana, half the average salary in France. At the end of the twentieth century, two-thirds of the active population find work in administration (the tertiary sector), a much smaller percentage work in industries that transform raw materials into products (the secondary sector), and less than ten percent work in production—agriculture, fishing, wood industry, mining (the primary sector). These percentages represent a dramatic change when compared to post World War II figures indicating 60% involved in production, the primary sector. Leaders of Guiana face the challenge of finding solutions to this imbalance in the work force. With imports far outdistancing exports, the economy has been dependent upon metropolitan France and must change so that people produce more goods for local consumption or more exports. Different ethnic groups tend to favor one particular facet of the economy over another (for example, a majority of the Hmong choose agriculture), suggesting the possibility of certain groups being more prone to economic difficulties. However, high unemployment affects all populations in Guiana, making public assistance necessary for people representing each segment (Delannon, "Réalité").

Important areas for both the present economy and future development exist in agriculture, fishing and aquaculture, forestry, mining, tourism, and the space center. Significant exports are fish, shrimp, rice, wood, and gold with the majority going to France, including Martinique and Guadeloupe, and countries of the European Union. Major imports are food products and fuel (France, French Embassy 8). Construction of Petit-Saut, the hydroelectric power dam on the Sinnamary River, is expected to decrease the need for dependency on others for power. At the same time, however, it has raised grave concerns about the ecological cost of flooding such a large area of the forest (Guyane, Conseil Général 167). One would expect issues of diversity to be less apparent between different ethnic groups when considering the economic situation except, perhaps, when concerns of pollution arise. Groups of people living in direct contact with the environment are more apt to protest dramatic changes to their physical world.

Agriculture exists both in the early Amerindian tradition of burning small areas, planting, harvesting, and moving to another space while the original rejuvenates, and on the modern level of the rice industry where research and technological advances increase productivity and quality. Other agricultural products with a promising future are pineapples and manioc (cassava). As for the fishing industry, royal shrimp from Guiana enjoy great distinction in the European market as well as in the United States and Japan. Fishing provides another major export, but must compete with countries in which production costs are lower (Mouren-Lascaux 114–121).

Wood products have experienced a highly fluctuating success rate due to increased construction in Guiana for the space center and stiff competition in the world market from Brazil. However, that industry remains a strong possibility for increased wood product manufacturing when it solves problems of harvesting. As the forest becomes more accessible, scientists share the environment with the wood industry for medical research and the discovery of new plants, insects, and mammals. A 1988 film—"Un radeau des cimes" produced by the French Institute for Scientific Research for Cooperative Development (ORSTOM)—shows how scientists discover new plant species by studying the treetops from a "raft" constructed at the summits of trees. Transportation to and from this research station is by hot air balloon (Mouren-Lascaux 95).

The mining industry has continued since the first discovery of gold in 1854, although individual prospectors encounter serious disadvantages when competing against multinational companies with their modern equipment for extracting gold. Some of the gold finds its way to artisans who craft high quality jewelry. Future mining possibilities include deposits of copper, diamonds, uranium, lead, zinc, silver, and other mineral natural resources (Mouren-Lascaux 123).

The space center at Kourou, discussed previously, also contributes significantly to the economy. It imports space scientists to live in the community and employs workers to build and maintain structures. Financed and run by France and other European countries, launchings of the rocket Ariane bring both financial investments and a more positive image to this land (Bordry 14).

Finally, tourism holds strong possibilities for future development. Although less developed in Guiana than in other countries of the Caribbean region, it attracts approximately 20,000 tourists per year (France, French Embassy 13). Never benefiting from a reputation as a new world paradise as did its sister departments in the Antilles, Guiana is becoming known for "adventure" vacations where hardy tourists can explore rivers with their challenging rapids and waterfalls and the forest with expert guides, discovering the myriad unusual species of flora and fauna. This type of clientele is interested in "eco-tourism." More controversial are visits to Amerindian villages to observe cultures that have chosen not to accept a technologically influenced lifestyle (Mouren-Lascaux 121–122). Although Guiana does not possess the same number of miles of sandy idyllic beaches as Martinique and Guadeloupe, her beaches offer encounters with oceanic wild fowl and marine animals. Tourists can observe the egg laying ritual of giant Luth turtles, coming from the ocean each year as they have over the centuries (Sanité 20).   Reading a tourist guide of Guiana entices travelers looking for unusual experiences not available in conventional holidays.

With the possibilities of growth in these industries comes the concern of Guianese leaders for ecologically sound management—from the selection of trees in the Amazon forest to fishing methods in the ocean. Some concerned citizens also express the belief that research should be conducted to verify that pollution from the space center is not adversely affecting the health of the population or the ecosystem of the surrounding area. Conferences run by Guianese leaders in conjunction with researchers from around the world indicate a growing concern for the ecology of the area. They advocate policies to protect the environment while still promoting progress for the economy.   One such colloquium on Amazonian ecological development took place in Cayenne in 1991 between scientists, administrators, and other interested parties from Guiana and Brazil. The main thrust of this conference highlighted the fact that the peoples of the Amazon region consider themselves both qualified and entitled to determine practices that would protect their territories from environmental destruction. Interestingly enough, this conference preceded by one year the highly publicized and well-represented 1992 international conference on the environment in Rio de Janeiro. Conclusions from these kinds of conferences express the belief that sound ecological practices must become an integral part of economic and educational development (Guyane, Conseil Général 179–180).

Culture

Being a part of France, the educational system in Guiana follows that of the rest of the country, a centralized organization directed by the Ministry of Education. The Antilles-Guiana Directorate of Education established in 1974 directly administers educational services for Guiana (France, French Embassy 11). However, as recently as 1996, demonstrations by students in Guiana indicated the need for local educational decisions and control, and more facilities for advanced education.

Primary and secondary schools prepare students for the "baccalauréat" — a test taken upon completion of high school and necessary for admission to French universities. In 1993, 72 elementary and 18 public secondary schools existed to educate more than 34,000 school-age children who made up 30% of the population (France, French Embassy 11). Because census figures cannot be accurate due to the frequency of illegal immigration, the literacy rate given in 1992 as 83% can only be an estimate. With rapidly increasing numbers of students, authorities recognize the need to build more schools and to adapt the content of teaching for the new school population. Between 1982 and 1990, this population more than doubled, increasing costs and challenges in meeting needs of children of recent immigrants.

Differences in educational levels between children and parents can create generational conflict, but the continued importance of children and attention to them in the Guianese culture mitigate some of these problems. The department addressed one discrepancy in opportunity between urban and rural areas in 1986 by financing a library service to rural communities, establishing a network of rural libraries and a library bus service (*Ruralité* 34–36). Augmented library services and availability of adult education help bridge gaps created by disparities in educational levels within the family and community.

Government regulations require students to attend school until they are sixteen. Those who choose to continue their education in Guiana have technical schooling at hand with professional training available in agriculture, construction, public works, mechanical and electrical engineering, electronics and refrigeration (France, French Embassy 11). Local teacher training schools prepare students for teaching posts at the primary level. The Académie de Guyane, created in Cayenne from a former education nucleus and expanded in 1997, offers studies leading to the equivalent of a bachelor's degree, after which students can pursue further schooling in Martinique or metropolitan France. The Université des Antilles-Guyane in Martinique confers degrees in law and economics, humanities, physics, biology, and medical science (Guyane, OCCE). Students can also attend the Institute of Technology (IUT). Students from Guiana often choose to continue their studies in metropolitan France. Many of them do not return.

With educational opportunities in Guiana came the evolution of a rich heritage in literature. The first recorded author, Alfred Parepou, published a novel *Atipa* in 1885. However, literary history does not indicate his ethnic background nor his position in society (Rouch 219). Most Guianese authors in the twentieth century spent some time in metropolitan France, usually for schooling. René Maran (1887–1960) attended school in Bordeaux through his high school years, but did not have the financial resources to continue university studies. He took a job in Africa, and wrote there until his remarkable entry into the French literary world winning the Prix Goncourt in 1921 for his novel *Batouala*. At that time in history, Parisian literary circles did not expect a black writer to be recognized by such a prestigious prize (Rouch 219, 229).

Assuredly the most influential literary giant from French Guiana remains Léon-Gontran Damas (1912–1978), a poet, politician, cultural ambassador, teacher, lecturer, and scholar recognized and admired throughout the world. Aimé Césaire (Martinique), Léopold Sédar Senghor (Senegal), and Damas created the Négritude movement in the 1930s while all three were students in Paris. Damas was recognized for denouncing the causes of alienation suffered by Blacks. Through his poetry, he was forthright in his condemnation of the colonial experience. His poems, marked by a striking rhythm sometimes compared to the beat of the African tam-tam, express anger at oppression by colonizers and pride in a heritage with roots in Africa's past. His interest in the African diaspora endured throughout his life, taking him for extended stays to France, various African countries, Brazil, Canada, and the United States. Damas spent his final years lecturing around the world and teaching courses at Howard University in Washington, D.C. (Racine 25–54).

Important writers following Damas include Bertène Juminer (1927–), novelist and physician, professor in the medical school and rector of the Université Antilles-Guyane, Élie Stephenson (1944–), poet, playwright, teacher, economist, Serge Patient, poet and novelist, Claudy Patrick (born Patrick Langlois, 1949–), poet, novelist, artist, musician, and authors/poets René Jadfard, Gilles Sirder, Michel Alimeck, Christian Rollé, Raoul-Philippe Danaho (Rouch 219–232). Guianese writers are often grouped with other Caribbean authors. However, when studying their literary works, students should remember differences in life experiences that mark psychological development and therefore the author's perspective.

These authors wrote in French, reaching a wider audience, but also incorporated some Creole into their poems or dialogues. French is the language of most literature, education, administration, and "official" economic activity. However, languages in Guiana are as diverse as the population: several Amerindian languages, other languages spoken by the "implanted" groups (Hmong, Surinamese, Brazilians) and last but not least, Creole, the most commonly spoken language. The language of "amour," Creole is used by mothers for expressing tenderness to their children (Mouren-Lascaux 75). Creole in Guiana is similar to that spoken in other francophone regions. An outsider recognizes some resemblance to French but finds it difficult to follow a conversation. Examples of Creole:

English	Creole	French
Hello, how are you?	kouman to fika?	Comment ça va?
I'm fine	mo la ka gadé to	Je vais bien.
Thank you	grenmsi	Merci beaucoup.
Where are you going?	Koté to k'alé?	Où vas-tu?
Excuse me	eskizé mo	Excuse-moi.
Goodbye	maché bien / tchinbé rèd	Au revoir.

In the past, educated members of the society regarded Creole in a negative light, associating it with illiteracy. They considered Creole to be broken French. People no longer judge Creole as "bad" French, but as the legitimate oral expression of people of the Caribbean region. Each group tends to emphasize the differences in vocabulary and pronunciation that distinguish their version from the others. Generally, however, these are only nuances and Creole is understood by all. Professors now teach it at the Université des Antilles et de la Guyane in Fort-de-France, Martinique. Thus, literature and educational systems valorize this language which has always been spoken within the family.

The Creole family, a very close-knit unit in Guiana, tends to be the extended type. This means that three, sometimes even four generations may live in the same household. Children can live with relatives for various reasons without any "formal" arrangements. Because older members remain important to the family, their living quarters do not necessarily change as they age. Senior citizen housing is a new concept in Guiana, with only two or three such facilities in existence. Young people do not generally rent apartments, remaining "at home" until they get married, regardless of their age. While some of the young people who have studied and lived abroad may prefer to live on their own, financial conditions often force them to return to the extended family.

The family unit usually revolves around the mother and her pivotal role cannot be overemphasized. Known for her intense love and affection for her children, the Guianese woman is also the undisputed authority figure. Marriage is generally not considered necessary for raising children. Approximately 50% of children are born to parents who are not married and children may or may not know their father. This fact does not matter, as there is no social stigma attached to single parenting.

The Guianese family is said to be hyper-protective of its young members (Delannon, "Réalité"). Perhaps this can be explained by the fact that there are always grandparents, aunts, uncles, and cousins around to share life, creating the ultimate haven for children. The impact of losing a parent, for example, is not as great as in places without this type of strong family network. This system provides emotional stability so that even in the more difficult economic circumstances, children are cared for and seem to have a happy childhood.

Families enjoy music and dancing, an important form of expression for people of all ages. Traditionally, African based rhythms from other parts of the Caribbean such as Guadeloupe, Martinique, Haiti, Dominica, and Trinidad, have influenced the music. Similarly, dances such as the rhythmic "béguine" from Guadeloupe are popular, especially among the less young. In the 1990s, popular music was heavily influenced by the following: rap from North America, reggae from Jamaica, and raga from the West Indian islands. Younger people seem to identify with this music which is an interesting cultural hybrid. Because the rhythms are so similar to the music being produced in North America and in the Caribbean region, one sometimes needs to listen closely in order to recognize that it is being sung in French.

In contrast to one or two week celebrations of Carnival in other parts of the world, Guiana enjoys the Carnival season from Epiphany (January 6) to Ash Wednesday (five to eight weeks). Critics complain that the duration paralyzes the country. It is the time when nothing else can compete for the attention of the minds of most of the people in Cayenne. Some claim that productivity suffers whether in the workplace or at school because of the intense activity involved in preparing for and participating in Carnival. Others see it as a very cohesive force that encourages people across generations and economic divisions to spend time together enjoying and reinforcing their cultural heritage.

Regardless of one's point of view, no one can deny the positive influence of this season with its spirited time of music and dancing in the streets. Those who can afford the materials create colorful costumes. Those who cannot are not left out; they can enjoy Carnival by simply painting themselves with mud. In this sense, it is a time when economic and other social barriers are completely broken down—everyone is welcome and expected to participate with true equality. Such an approach to celebration reinforces the feeling of harmony between ethnic groups choosing to participate, bringing together diverse groups in common entertainment.

Women play a very important role during this season by creating costumes with some unique disguises made for women by women. Behind their masks, women clearly have the upper hand in some of the "games" played. They can tease men without being recognized and then deny participating in the Carnival. Men cannot prove their participation because the costumes are prepared in utmost secrecy. Accompanied by the rhythmic music and dancing, this type of flirting can be misconstrued by outsiders as bordering on promiscuity.

Many kinds of food are evident year round, not only during the Carnival season, because of the tropical climate and different cooking styles from the variety of ethnic groups. Cooks around the world know Guiana for its "Cayenne" pepper, serving as an indicator of the spicy nature of its cuisine. A great variety of dishes can be found, including the use of many different vegetables, meat, fish, seafood, fowl, and tropical game. Most of the vegetables used in Guiana are fairly well known, such as eggplant, cucumbers, green beans, but other less known tropical vegetables are also used (okra and manioc). Some of the fruits grown in Guiana are known around the world: coconut, mango, guava, pineapple, papaya. Others not well known outside the Caribbean region include soursop, West Indian cherries, sugar apples, monkey apples, awara.

Soursop is a very fleshy fruit with many seeds that resemble watermelon seeds. About the size of a large cantaloupe but elongated in shape, the fruit's flesh is milky white and delicious eaten by itself. One can also remove the seeds and blend the flesh with milk, cinnamon, and sugar to make a refreshing drink. The West Indian cherry is similar to cherries found in North America. The color varies from pink to bright red, but when overripe, it becomes dark red like the North American black cherry. Although the same size or slightly smaller, it is distinctly different in flavor. The seeds, also different in appearance, tend to be in clusters with each segment resembling a flake of oatmeal.

The awara, a deep orange fruit about the size of a small nectarine, has a moist and slightly stringy flesh. When children eat the flesh of the awara, a temporary orange tinge is left on the fingers and teeth. The flesh of the awara is used as the base for a type of soup or stew, "bouillon d'awara" which is very popular at Easter time. This meal is made with several types of meat, poultry and vegetables and takes two to three days to prepare.

Prospects

Political status notwithstanding, Guiana clearly has a very distinct culture. Several groups of people coexist in spite of marked differences in origin, and each group is proud of its heritage. The Amerindians who were the first known inhabitants have lived in harmony with nature by carrying out what are now known to be ecologically sound practices. The Alukus, also close to nature, have maintained their African ancestral heritage by living far away from the French influence. The Creoles advocate a "melting pot" or "créolisation" of all the peoples of Guiana into one homogenous group, and because they are the established majority bring political pressure to this end.

Regardless of origin, the Guianese people working together can constitute a formidable force, one with the power to bargain with the national government and therefore determine their future. The overriding authority of the metropolitan French government serves as another force to unify the many different cultural constituents, because only through unity can they garner enough strength to influence French politics for the good of the whole department. The new wave of awareness that is emerging from young people representing all of the various groups and the desire many of them share to work toward being one, will allow Guiana to realize its full potential. Perhaps this land with its mosaic of inhabitants will serve as a model of peaceful coexistence.

NOTES

1.   A department is an administrative division of France. There are 95 departments in metropolitan France and four overseas departments (Martinique, Guadeloupe, Guiana, and Reunion). One can compare a French overseas department and its relationship to France to a state like Hawaii and its relationship to the United States.

2.   Colonial powers eventually divided this plateau into three territories: British Guiana is now independent of Britain and called Guyana. Dutch Guiana, also independent, changed its name to Surinam, and French Guiana (la Guyane Française) remains a department of France.

REFERENCES

Bordry, Olivier, Jean-Pierre Bove et Valérie Lambert, eds. *La Guyane dans l'Union européenne*. Luxembourg: OPOCE, 1994.

Delannon, Roland. *Conquérir Cayenne au féminin: L'Election de Christiane Taubira-Delannon aux législatives de mars 1993*. Matoury, Guiana: Imprimerie R.G.I., 1993.

——. "La Réalité guyanaise." Le Cercle Français. University of Wisconsin-Stevens Point. 14 Apr. 1997.

France. French Embassy. *French Guiana: A Geographical and Historical Survey*. Washington: French Embassy Press, 1993.

Guyane. Conseil Général. Actes du colloque éco-développement amazonien: Traditions et environnement. Proc. of a Conference on the environment of the Amazon, 19-21 Apr. 1991. Cayenne: Imprimerie Départementale, 1991.

Guyane. OCCE (Office de la Coopération et du Commerce Extérieur). *Agriculture, aperçu historique, centre spatial, commerce, éducation, emploi, forêt, industries, organisation politique, pêche, population, santé, situation*. Cayenne: n.d.

Mouren-Lascaux, Patrice. *La Guyane*. Paris: Karthala, 1990.

Papillon. Dir. Robert Dorfmann and Franklin J. Schaffner. Perf. Steve McQueen and Dustin Hoffman. Based on book by Henri Charrière. Warner Home Video, 1973.

Racine, Daniel. *Léon-Gontran Damas: L'Homme et l'oeuvre*. Paris: Présence Africaine, 1983.

Rivière, Léon, ed. *Destination Guyane: Guide pratique tourisme et loisirs en Guyane française*. Cayenne: Outre Mer Editions, n.d.

Rouch, Alain and Gérard Clavreuil. *Littératures nationales d'écriture française: Afrique noire, Caraïbes, Océan Indien*. Paris: Bordas, 1987.

La Ruralité et le développement économique: Mana. Proc. of a Conference on rurality and economical development. 7 July 1991. Mana, Guiana: 1991.

Sanité, Léon P. *Conservation et gestion du patrimoine naturel guyanais*. Cayenne: Sepanguy, 1995.

Taubira-Delannon, Christiane. *Cap sur l'horizon*. Belem, Brazil: Cejup Graficentro, 1992.

DISCUSSION QUESTIONS

1. What aspects of Guiana's history have contributed to its present day diversity?

2. Explain the hypothesis that the attitude of freed slaves was affected by observing the treatment of white prisoners. What strengths or weaknesses do you find in this hypothesis?

3. Develop some possible reasons why all the different Amerindian groups did not unite to resist the Europeans.

4. Discuss possible ramifications of a sudden increase in population from 65,000 to 95,000, not through birth but through an immigration plan devised by France's government.

5. Suggest several reasons for such a large concentration of the population along the coastal strip.

6. Compare histories of indigenous people of Guiana and native peoples of North America.

7. What contributed to Guiana's negative image in the past? Why is this image becoming more positive?

8. Who were the maroons? Discuss their political evolution.

9. How did some slaves react against their enslavement? Have you heard of other techniques of resistance used by slaves?

10. Explain the original intent of the penal colony and what actually happened. If you have seen the movie *Papillon* with Dustin Hoffman and Steve McQueen, describe the events and the terrain.

11. Explain the possible irony of a young man from Guiana becoming a soldier to fight for France in World War I.

12. Explain some differences between the status as a colony versus a department of France.

13. Name the ethnic groups that make up the population and discuss reasons for their presence.

14. Develop arguments for and against Guiana's independence from France. Form two groups—those for independence and those wishing to remain a department. Present your arguments, supporting them with examples when possible.

15. Is it important for the people of Guiana to produce more goods? Why or why not?

16. Discuss pros and cons for the construction of a hydroelectric power dam.

17. The forest in Guiana forms part of the Amazon forest. What promises does it hold for the economy? What are issues for and against its development?

18. Choose one facet of Guiana's economy (agriculture, fishing, forestry, mining, tourism, space center) and explain its possibilities for growth and difficulties to overcome.

19. Some groups of people in Guiana are concerned about ecological problems inherent in an economy of growth. Given the list of industries (#18), what problems might one anticipate?

20. Read a poem by Léon-Gontran Damas aloud. Discuss its rhythm and its meaning.

21. Discuss possible advantages and disadvantages of living together within a large extended family unit.

22. Listen to music from Guiana or the Caribbean and compare it to music one can hear in the U.S. Do you hear similarities? Differences? Your library may have examples of music from different regions in the world.

23. Have you visited a city where the Carnival season is celebrated? Describe the events, costumes, formal and informal activities you observed.

24. Explain why you think there is more harmony among the different ethnic groups in Guiana than what one often finds around the world.

PART FOUR

Francophone Issues in North America

❖ CHAPTER EIGHT

"Je me souviens": *-I remember*
Quebec's Literary and Linguistic Journey

Marie-Paule Méda

French as a world entity has acquired a status and a new scope that were not foreseeable a century and a half ago. It has been bestowed with a fashionable designation, *"la francophonie"* to signify this new wordly situation. For several decades now, the phenomenon of *la francophonie* or the French-speaking world community, has introduced new and unprecedented levels of linguistic consciousness in Quebec in particular, as well as the other French localities in Canada. French and Frenchness *à la Québécois* are being reaffirmed as well as preserved through new laws, and greater efforts are being made to guard them both from the global predominance and invasion of the English language.

In this essay, the evolution of Quebec as a distinctive society and culture will be examined through its portrayal in the francophone literature, music, and films which have proliferated throughout Canada as well as the rest of the world. The significance of Quebec's unique historical past figures in the making of its literary discourse, which, before 1950 was traditional in its retro/ introspection of those former times. However with the *Révolution tranquille*, all of that changed dramatically, and the *Québécois* people were able to transcend this attachment to their valorous past without ever forgetting it. For the past embodied their distinctiveness as a founding culture, which is now a minority in an anglophone sea.

The French language and culture have been a part of Canada ever since the origins of the country, in 1534, with Jacques Cartier who took possession of this new land in the name of François the 1st of France. French became an official language in Canada in 1969, due mostly to the fact that for some time, Quebec had been asserting its independence as a province, and also as a people. The then Prime Minister, Pierre-Elliot Trudeau, a francophone native of Québec, had been a strong advocate of the notion of bilingualism, sensing its merits for the whole nation.

The Origins of a New Society

Already before the British conquest of New France in 1763, a new society, influenced by the French Regime elite class who was then governing, had been emerging slowly. All of the colonists coming to the new country were of the Roman Catholic Church, since a decree from France's statesman Cardinal Richelieu in 1627 had prevented Huguenots or Jews from emigrating to the colony (Jack 59). Education was mainly under the Roman Catholic Church's rule and was available chiefly in urban centers such as Quebec City and Montreal. Education was mostly limited to elementary instruction where boys were instructed by male clergy and girls by Ursuline nuns. At the superior level, there existed one college where liberal arts were taught, the Quebec Seminary which was established in 1663 and was affiliated with the main Jesuit college. The natural heir to the Seminary was the University of Laval, founded in 1852, which later opened a subsidiary in Montreal in 1878, and which became the University of Montreal in 1920.

During this period, the local literary production was essentially limited to historical publications including those of Samuel de Champlain, the Jesuits, and the Franciscan Gabriel Sagard, and to a few occasional poems and songs (Jack 95). But because the king had forbidden the setting up of presses in the colony, all printing was done from France (Tétu de Labsade 412). Nevertheless, the first colonists loved to read, and around 1605, Marc Lescarbot, a Parisian lawyer who wrote *Une histoire de la Nouvelle-France* as well as poems, opened the first bookstore in Port Royal, Acadia (the very first French founded settlement) (Jack 64-65; Tétu de Labsade 436).

The English Regime and Its Influence

After the British conquest in 1763, French Canada was indeed a very poor colony in many ways. Most of the properties near Quebec and Montreal had been burned down or appropriated by the English army. The inhabitants were uncertain and dispirited. They bore no trust in the new government and feared losing forever their customs, their language, and their autonomy, especially since the memory of the Acadian deportation between 1755 and 1762 was still fresh in their minds.

As for the British they were rather perplexed by what they found in the new colony. Convinced that they would be dealing with a backward population, they had encountered instead a high society of polished aristocrats and their ladies, all dressed in the latest French fashions, enjoying the high life. Unfortunately, this upper class decorum was not to persist much longer, as most of the upper crust chose to leave the country altogether after the arrival of the British. The Jesuits and the Recollets were ordered out of the country by the English who feared their influence and while these orders returned in the mid-nineteenth century, their departure left behind only the Sulpicians and a layer of the society, which was in many instances, illiterate, disheartened, and often living in isolation in the countryside.

Because of their illiteracy, their seclusion, and their love of agriculture—a way of life encouraged and even advocated by the remaining Church—the French-speaking population became further anchored in the remembrance of their origins and customs. Yet while embodying but a human toll among the English, the French colonists appeared to be dismissing the fact that they were the conquered ones and anticipated that newcomers to their agricultural world would assimilate to their lifestyle, whether they came from France or elsewhere. In fact, with time, their population actually surpassed that of the English, and a later agreement, the 1774 Quebec Act (in opposition to the 1763 Paris Treaty) permitted the more numerous French colonists the continuance of the profession of their faith, the use of the French language, and the option of trial under the Paris civil law system. This agreement thus set in ink the distinction of the French Canadian society.

French Canada Acquires a Culture of Its Own

The actual publication of the first book in French Canada happened in 1830, *Épitres, satires, chansons, épigrammes et d'autres pièces de vers* by Michel Bibaud, a newspaper owner. Since printing in New France had been prohibited under the French Regime, books brought back from France oftentimes faced the reproof of the Church as being too liberal, and therefore nocuous to the mind. Notwithstanding, bookstores and libraries sprang up as time went by. In 1796, a public library was inaugurated in Montreal and two new bookstores, Garneau and Crémazie, opened their doors in 1844 in Quebec City. A great many historical accounts of actual conditions and tribulations in Canada, including travels, explorations, and the way of life in the new colony were published by travelers, explorers, historians, nuns, and other clerics (Jack 65), thus providing a link beween the two eras. One of the major writings of historical and cultural substance was the *Histoire du Canada* (written between 1845–52) by François-Xavier Garneau, considered to be the first national historian of Quebec. It was written in rebuttal to Lord Durham's 1839 deprecative report after the Patriots' rebellion of 1837–38, which declared that the French Canadians were a people without history or literature (Tétu de Labsade 413).

The very first novels (in the broadest sense of the word) in French Canada, depicted stories about robbers and fantastic adventures. With the Patriots' rebellion still fresh in their minds, and the remnants of anarchy still lingering, French Canadian writers displayed a propensity for evasion through the unusual in their works. Nonetheless, a certain surge in other forms of literary production was also experienced; the publication of poems and of historical, sociological, and naturalist novels was increasingly manifest. *Les anciens Canadiens* by Philippe Aubert de Gaspé, the Elder, considered the earliest French Canadian novel by some researchers, was essentially a factual portrait of life in society and in nature. It was a novel of manners written in 1863, in which scenes of the times of the British Conquest were intermixed with French Canadian legends and typical descriptions of climatic conditions such as the breaking up of ice blocks on the St-Lawrence (Tétu de Labsade 414). Then followed the trend of idealistic novels, where the author would write in great detail of the beauty and benefits of rural life. There were no great tragedies or sorrows, rather the simple, domestic joys that the land procures. One such author Antoine Gérin-Lajoie wrote *Jean Rivard, le défricheur (récit de la vie réelle)*. As the title indicates [*Jean Rivard, the Pioneer (A Story of Real Life)*], only true facts were to be portrayed, just as the Church would have liked it. This was a very important factor in early French Canadian literature since authors could easily be blacklisted if they did not conform to the social criteria of the times.

In the nineteenth century, matriarchy experienced a significant boost of power. Still the traditional role assigned to women, that of spouse, childbearer, nurturer, and housewife, remained the norm (Tétu de Labsade 71). Nonetheless, a few women writers broke away from this established pattern and swayed the rules by publishing literary works, mostly novels. Laure Conan (real name, Félicité Angers) was one of the first ones to do so. She published the first novel with a psychological propensity, *Angéline de Montbrun* (1884), which provoked critical argumentation for its multiple interpretations, voices, and relationships. The story, by mixing epistolary, third person narration, and diary modes, led to ambiguity and confused the role of the traditional narrator. It left far too many hiatuses to be filled by the reader. Angéline's problematic relationship with her father, her fiancé Maurice, and with her own analytical self further complicated the issue of individual happiness and the status of women as a whole (Jack 70).

Although literature was establishing itself as a worthwhile cultural tradition, the long-standing oral institution of French Canada remained the substantial source of communication throughout the colony since its origins. As a matter of fact, the spoken word was the only way to communicate with one another in rural areas. Thus, through songs, stories, and legends were transmitted the language, culture, and traditions of an isolated people confined mostly to their homes and communities. Legends, in particular, proved oftentimes to be the most important form of entertainment, whether at celebrations, at family reunions, or at fortuitous gatherings. Their vast popularity was possibly due to the inherent element of magic that always seemed to accompany them and that brought just the appropriate exotic touch to the inhabitants' secluded lives. This legacy passed down from generation to generation was truly a rich one, and was compiled in anthologies by researchers and historians as early as the end of the nineteenth century for anyone to read (Tétu de Labsade 415).

However, it is poetry which dominated most of nineteenth-century literature after the Rebellion. In 1860, a literary school emerged (*l'École littéraire et patriotique de Québec*) led by the abbot Henri-Raymond Casgrain, a man of the church who loved to tell stories and to engage in some literary theory. France's influence, even from afar, was felt through the literary world. Louis Fréchette, who borrowed from Victor Hugo some of his stylistic effects, and Octave Crémazie, who conformed to the Romantic literary movement in France, were two of the most known poets of the time. Two decades later, came the literary school of Montreal (*l'École littéraire de Montréal*), a serious group who met to work privately but who also provided open work sessions. The school lasted about thirty years. One of its most famous poets was Émile Nelligan (1879–1941), the classic accursed poet (*le poète maudit*). Born of a French Canadian mother and an Irish father, Nelligan was not a happy child and never got along with his father, while he dearly loved his mother. He was very much influenced by Verlaine and the Belgian symbolists, refusing to heed political and religious issues. Even so, his poems portray "a refusal of the doctrinaire, of narrow prescriptions, and are concerned instead with inner experience, with spirituality, with the importance of the individual, and with the power of language [...]" (Jack 67). Nelligan wrote his poems at a very young age between 1896–98. Unfortunately shortly thereafter, he sank into madness at the age of twenty years old and never wrote again. Still his legacy is a profound and unforgettable one. "The Mind's Moonlight" from *Selected Poems* is a fine example of his work; it traces the spiritual path of his thoughts and portrays an illusory world with a surrealist aura.

Breaking Away from Traditional Patterns

On the whole, however, literature at the end of the nineteenth century dismissed with the socio-economic realities of the times as well as the evolutionary, creative European spirit. Much of this tendency was a product of the Church's reluctance to recognize revolutionary French and European esthetics. Many works were censured because of the perceived liberalism and radicalism expressed in them. Thus, the true state of the *Québécois* people's life was denied by the constant recall of past happenings through tales of adventure and the idealization of country life. Mostly memories of an era when men were soldiering or farming only were depicted. The progress of industrialization and urbanization was largely ignored. It was an elitist literature advocating an isolated, withdrawn people who remained dependent upon idyllic former times and ways.

From the beginning of the twentieth century until the Second World War the same themes of traditional values and regionalism, and of glorification of the past and the land, still governed the literature. This was the literature of a colonized and subdued people who ignored the surrounding world and its reality. Nevertheless, a few novels left an imprint and announced the winds of change on the horizon. One such novel, considered one of the greatest literary successes of the times, was *Maria Chapdelaine* (France 1914; Canada 1916) by a French author, Louis Hémon. To the eyes of his French compatriots, the novel depicted with love and respect a vibrant and fascinating French nation outside of France. Hémon's novel was at first dismissed by the French Canadian society as foreign and portraying an image of a country locked in its traditions; yet, his depiction of the pioneering spirit of the Quebec people resistant to the exterior forces of change was later viewed as accurate (Joubert 324).

Hémon, who had resided in the province of Quebec for about two years before writing his novel, chose to relate the story of a fictive family, the Chapdelaines. They embodied the historical determinism of the Quebec people, reflected in the idealistic notion of never abandoning the soil they had come to colonize, raising a family, and living as Christians, for this was their destiny. Although the novel revealed the traditional themes of the times, such as the love for nomadic freedom (François Paradis), the insidious temptations of the city (Lorenzo Surprenant), and the enduring love for the land (Eutrope Gagnon), it manages to convey the character and local flavor of the protagonists' lives in a way that is neither exotic nor banal. The Chapdelaine patriarch, for example, was always on the move and always ready to start again instead of remaining on the same piece of land as the church advocated. Realistic in a romantic way, the characters were nevertheless believable and enticing to readers. In certain passages from the book, the reader can witness how much the French Canadian society feared the exterior world seeking to invade the narrowness of their environment. Here, Mother Chapdelaine is viewed as the keeper of the traditional way of life and specifically of the French language, while Lorenzo Surprenant, who embodies the "betrayer of tradition," chose exile to the "States" for better wages and quality of life.

Even so, the vogue of mythifying and glorifying the soil was not a concept impartially accepted by all writers. Albert Laberge, author of *La Scouine* (1918), could be characterized as a detractor from this trend. His avant-garde novel showed, in a crude and even frightening portrayal, the intellectual mediocrity and physical hardship existing in rural Quebec. It absolutely revoked the myth of happiness and solace in the way of life praised and extolled as best by the Church and the elite. From the early thirties to the end of the Second World War, novels started to move away from this idealization of the land and its fetishism to a more honest realism. Protagonists were now representing unusual themes such as exile, instability, or a certain fundamental madness, typifying new visions about rural communities. Novelists such as Claude-Henri Grignon, Félix-Antoine Savard, Ringuet, and Germaine Guèvremont were still dealing with the traditional themes of the Quebec soil, but their books were turning away from the age-old concept of conservative and idealistic nationalism. However, Jean-Charles Harvey was the first to use the city as a backdrop for his book *Demi-Civilisés* as early as 1934 and shocked the authorities, especially the Church which promptly chastised him from the pulpit. He subsequently lost his job as the editor-in-chief of the newspaper *Le Soleil*.

Poetry also was shifting away from the old topics and flirting with new ideas. An elitist literature more so than the popular novel, poetry was now embracing universalism, lyricism, and social panoramas. Poets were contemplating humanism and originality, rather than politics, history, and ideology, and were trying to find new and different ways of expressing themselves, often looking to French contemporary literature for meaning and sense. Hector de Saint-Denys Garneau's works were spiritual and personal, but at the same time inscribed with the unfamiliar and exceptional. Alain Grandbois imprinted his poems with his travels, the dream world, and his transcendental quest of the absolute, rendering a poetry that is reminiscent of Cendrars, Claudel, and Saint-John de Perse (Joubert 324).

The Second World War years were frenetic ones, for almost overnight, Quebec saw itself promoted to the position of editing agent for the French publishers, with the Nazi occupation having more or less stopped all possible publishing activity. Numerous publishing houses appeared, and French writers and poets that had been censured before, including Rimbaud, Gide, Bernanos, and others predating them, were now published and vastly read. These books were sold globally, but especially in South America, Australia, and of course, the U.S. This entire line of action benefited Quebec as a whole, encouraging newspapers to devote small sections to books and literature in general, which in turn prompted writers to open up to modernity.

Soon, novels published between 1941 and 1945, including Gabrielle Roy's *Bonheur d'occasion* (1945) and Roger Lemelin's *Au pied de la pente douce* (1944), were incorporating the city and its confined world into their panoramic perspective as urbanization was becoming a fact of reality. Another author, Robert Charbonneau, was the first to introduce the new psychological novel, while Yves Thériault acquainted his readers with a more pagan and wild nature. Novels were now importing the actual world into their narratives, as observed in *Bonheur d'occasion*. In the novel's story, a poor French Canadian family living in a poor district of Montreal is depicted realistically and dramatically. One particular scene represents an example of the breaks which were marring the familiar traditional way of life. The protagonist Eugene's will to enlist in the military typifies exile as a way of escaping a life no longer meaningful or even tolerable. But modernity and its effects were here to stay.

Paradoxically, an extreme lack of books was seen throughout the province, stemming in part from the fact that the clergy was still censuring all literature and dominating the school market, a lingering reminder of past tradition. The boom experienced during the war years because of the intermediary role of Quebec in the publishing business all but disappeared when the French publishers returned to the scene and monopolized the supply and demand again. The *Québécois* novel subsequently experienced a decrease in the number of works being written, but despite the limited volume of works produced, two distinct trends emerged during this time period. Some authors such as Roger Lemelin in his novel *Les Plouffe* (1948) and Gabrielle Roy in *Alexandre Chenevert* (1954) began to illustrate actuality and modernity in urban customs by dramatizing cities and their employees. The other trend was the psychological narrative, such as those of Anne Hébert in her works *Le Torrent*, (1950), *Les Chambres de bois* (1958), and André Giroux in his *Le Gouffre a toujours soif* (1953). André Langevin's *Poussière sur la ville* (1953) combined both trends and was very popular, while Yves Thériault gained international fame with his Inuit novel, *Agakuk* (1958).

Yet poetry fared better: it was published in greater numbers and its quality was notable. Somehow when change appeared on the horizon, a new wave of poetic verve unfolded, as if to lead the way to the forthcoming literary and cultural metamorphosis. In a similar fashion, a comparable trend had been experienced earlier in the life of the society, a sign that seemed to spell the desire to rise above tradition. Some well-known authors who announced changes in the wind were Alain Grandbois (*Rivages de l'homme*, 1948; *L'Étoile pourpre*, 1957); Anne Hébert (*Le Tombeau des rois*, 1953); and Rita Lasnier (*Présence de l'absence*, 1956).

Among the younger generation (such as Paul-Marie Lapointe, Roland Giguère, and Claude Gauvreau), one could observe the adoption of a new versification and a movement accentuating their philosophical, moral, and artistic views. It was a sort of contestation of the pre-established social and political order. Their poetry was purposefully modern, occult, and stimulating. Surrealist by inclination, Roland Giguère's poem "Landscape Adrift" from *Rose and Thorn, Selected Poems of Roland Giguère*, for example, displays a "lucid" strangeness. In this poem, there is a vivid sense of premonition of approaching changes, changes that will alter the familiar, the reliable notions, with a foreboding of future anxiety.

The *Révolution tranquille*

The *Révolution tranquille* [the Quiet Revolution, so-called because it did not engender fiery riots or disastrous dilemmas] marked the beginning of a new era for the province as well as for the arts in general. This period is usually associated with the death of Duplessis (1959), the then conservative and autoritorian Prime Minister of Quebec, who was opposed to all changes. A definite and much needed reform in the restructuring of the education system took place, stemming from the recommendations of the Parent Commission (1964) and effected by the Lesage liberal government. In it was a major shifting of control from the clerical to the secular and the implementation of *cégeps*—the result of the fusion of about forty classic colleges and normal schools between 1968–1970. A *cégep* is actually a college of general and professional teaching offering a diversified curriculum that allows students to choose different academic or technical avenues (Tétu de Labsade 190), and offers increased accessibility to university, post-secondary, and higher studies to everyone. What was reserved for a very small portion of the population was now open to a greater sector of the public, bringing about easier access and appreciation of books, music, theatres, museums, and the arts in general. In addition, a Department of Education was created from the Parent Commission's recommendations. Because a greater part of the population was educated, this further favored a stronger political and cultural commitment, as well as a keener sense of discernment and judgment in all other matters. Literature as well as the other arts experienced a steady expansion, if not always an even one. Cultural institutions were sprouting up everywhere: libraries, bookstores, publishing houses, theatres, and schools.

Writers, conscious of their narrow scopes, were impelled to examine their literary approaches. A brisk evolutionary movement rippled through all literary spheres, upsetting all previously established patterns. A new literature was emerging, and though it was still influenced by French trends and authors such as Colette, Gide, Mauriac, Malraux, and Camus, it remained fundamentally a *Québécois* literature with a definite new outlook. The poet Gaston Miron would write in 1957,

> Of course, we speak and write in French and our poetry will always be French poetry. That's understood. But you see, and it bears repeating, we are not French any more. Our attachment to the soil, our social mores, our mentalities are not the same any more.... If we wish to bring something to the French world and raise our poetry to the rank of the great national poetical writings, we must find ourselves, show our social distinction and our specific identity. (in Joubert 329, my translation)

One such author who chose to express a militant spirit in her work was Michèle Lalonde. She gained great attention in the early 1960s with her articles, essays, and poetic writings. In her poem, "Speak White," which essentially means "Speak English," she comes to the defense of the Quebec French and the feelings of the *Québécois* concerning their treatment as an underrated people. In *La Poésie québécoise*, Michelle Lalonde insists that the Quebec people understand and appreciate English in all its forms, even though they prefer their own tongue and their own literature. To illustrate her point, she juxtaposes English words with French ones, stressing the surrepticious invasion of English vocabulary into everyday life, as well as reinforcing at the same time the deterioration of the French language from this cohabitation.

Other authors, whether poets, novelists, or essayists, such as Jacques Godbout, Marie-Claire Blais, Hubert Aquin, Gérard Bessette, Gilles Marcotte, and Jean Rioux, likewise expressed their views through their works. Several literary reviews and journals were founded, including *Livres et auteurs québécois* (1963) which lasted for about twenty years. Others are still being published: *Liberté*, *Lettres québécoises*, *Spirale*, and *Nuit blanche*. Universities also came out with their own literary reviews, for example, *Études littéraires*, *Études françaises*, and *Voix et images*. All newspapers began to reserve a weekly section for literary and artistic purposes. Critical analysts, finding a greater and more eager readership, refined and redefined their judgments and standards, while a variety of essayists exposed their thoughts on various topics, covering literary and art theory, philosophy, sociology, cultural history, and politics, such as Gilles Marcotte, Jean Éthier-Blais, Jean Rioux, Jean Larose, and Pierre Vadeboncoeur to name but a few. In a passage from Jacques Godbout's *Hail Galarneau!*, which is the story of the tribulations of a fictive apprentice writer, François Galarneau, the protagonist's foremost effort in life is to "*vécrire*," and become an actual learning experience in living and writing. *Vécrire*, a neologism, is the juxtaposition of the verbs *vivre* and *écrire*—essentially to live and to write—, thus portraying, in a sense, this new *élan* for writing in Quebec:

> And I have visions like that, crowds of them, dreams that jostle each other in my attic. I know it's one of two things: you live or you write. I want to write *and* live. The best thing about that is that you're the boss, you're unemployed when you please, you hire yourself again, you drive off sad thoughts or you revel in them, you let yourself starve or you settle for words, but whatever you do it's your own idea. Words are worth more, in any case, than any kind of money. And there they are, piled up like cordwood in the dictionary. (Godbout 130-31)

From the 1960s on, novelists started breaking the traditional codes in writing, such as disrespecting chronology, mixing several point of views in one work, challenging authenticity, using *joual*, eroticism, and anarchistic protagonists opposed to order, religion, and morality. During those years, Quebec also witnessed an internationalization of its literature when several authors were chosen as recipients of French literary prizes. Marie-Claire Blais, for one, won the Prix Médicis for *Une saison dans la vie d'Émmanuel* (1966). (In the late 1940s Gabrielle Roy was the first writer to be awarded a French prize, the

Femina prize, for *Bonheur d'occasion*.) In the 1970s, a certain countercultural movement emerged whereby authors introduced in their stories topics such as sexual liberation, traveling as a means of pleasure, as well as the recourse to Oriental philosophies and drugs as experimental media. These practices defied traditional mores.

Furthermore, women were getting wider recognition; more of them were published, and around 1975, feminism emerged. Nicole Brossard, Madeleine Gagnon, France Théoret, Francine Noël, Yolande Villemaire, Louky Bersianik, and Denise Boucher were some of the writers who chose to interpret a more feminist picture of the modern *Québécoise* than was previously done. In the feminist oriented satire, *L'Euguélionne*, by Louky Bersianik, the author describes the saga of an extraterrestrial woman who comes to earth to observe our society. She discovers that half of the population is a superior half, and that both halves, the inferior and the superior, have somehow agreed to accept this improbable structure established by men. *L'Euguélionne*, the extraterrestrial woman declares: "A man in two is a woman."

Drama was slow to come into existence primarily because the Church viewed this type of cultural activity as harmful, but it definitely implanted itself in Quebec society once it acquired momentum. Ironically, it was a priest, Father Legault, who founded in the early 1940s the first theatre company, Les Compagnons du Saint-Laurent, whose first production in 1947 was Félix Leclerc's *Maluron* (Joubert 326). From this company came a great number of accomplished actors, comedians, producers, and stage designers. In 1948, Gratien Gélinas, a noted comedian, presented *Tit-Coq*, the first *Québécois* original drama of the twentieth century. Several theatre companies opened up thereafter, including Le Théâtre du Nouveau-Monde, le Rideau Vert, l'Égrégore and le Théâtre de Quat'sous, the last two being considered avant-garde in their production.

In the early 1970s, the issue of language was becoming more and more challenging to authors who wondered how they should express themselves in their novels, poems, and plays. Several started to favor the use of *le joual* (a relaxed form of French mixed with anglicisms, mispronunciations, and colloquialisms) as opposed to *Québécois* French (which differs from standard French mostly in its lexicon) as did Michel Tremblay, for one. He was the first to have written a play, *Les Belles-soeurs*, in *joual* and to have it performed in a theatre. While it proved to be an innovative way to stimulate the theatre, Tremblay's use of it was intended to express the confusion of a society he believed to be "without men," as were his plays. In his plays, he condemns the false virility of the *joual* language, this "'depraved linguistic sexuality' that poorly hides political powerlessness" (in Mailhot 112, my translation). Tremblay further declared: "We are a people that for many years has disguised itself to resemble another people... we have been transvestites for three hundred years" (in Mailhot 114, my translation). This use of the *joual* language in plays and novels lasted for about a dozen years, and the better known *joual* novels included *Le cassé* (Jacques Renaud), and *Le Cabochon* (André Major). Again according to Mailhot, the *joual* language was used also for political purposes, as a "structure of degeneration that denounces cultural, social and political bastardizing. [Its usage] is not to institutionalize a new language, nor a dialect, nor a *patois*, but an accent, a pronunciation, a certain lexicon; it is a pitiful, weak and sick state of French, a sub-language, [...] the language partly defeated of a defeated people [...]" (Mailhot 95-96, my translation). *Les Belles-Soeurs* by Michel Tremblay, a drama situated in East Montreal, tells the story of the everyday life of fifteen women who reveal unpleasant societal truths about blatant poverty, hatred, and moral indiscretions—mostly about one another—in a language that shocked some and pleased others.

Novels and plays were not the only means of cultural communication; both the radio and the television gained great popularity. Still, the radio was the first source of listening pleasure. It entertained the *Québécois* people with its broadcasts and popularized French Canadian music and songs since before World War I. Transmitted all over Quebec, radio reached remote regions where before no other contact with the exterior world had been really possible. It was in 1922 that a French radio station, CKAC, began transmitting in Montreal, and thereafter was followed by several others throughout the rest of the province. Until 1936 when *La Société Radio-Canada* was born, most stations were private businesses. Some diffused programs lasted up to thirty years, such as *Les belles histoires des pays d'en haut*—a spin-off serial story from *Un Homme et son péché* by Paul-Henri Grignon—, and *Les Joyeux troubadours*, a musical production. La Bolduc (Mary Travers), born of an Irish mother and a French Canadian father, was certainly one of the most popular and prolific singers of her era (1929–41). She lifted everyone's spirits—when global issues were not at their best—with her lively songs, performing on the radio as well as all over the province in all types of shows, including community centers, road tours, and even some night clubs.

French television made its debut in 1952 through Radio-Canada, and became a success overnight. It was a cultural phenomenon in and of itself: five years after its inception, most families had their own TV sets. Some programs, originating from popular novels (*Un Homme et son péché, Les Plouffe*), were so well liked that they lasted for years, with some series' characters even becoming household names. As the years went by, televised programs expanded to include a panorama of shows, including musicals, documentaries, films, and many other cultural offerings. Unfortunately, numerous American television channels soon started to invade the French Quebec television space, a cause of worry to the linguistic authorities and still a burning issue today.

Conversely, the appearance of the cinema industry was long in coming, due in part to the high costs of producing films, but also because the Church did not approve of this mode of representation. However, its rapid growth made up for the lost time: several *Québécois* and Canadian films gained international acclaim, among them, Claude Jutra's *Mon Oncle Antoine* and *Kamouraska*, Gilles Carle's *La vraie nature de Bernadette*, and Denys Arcand's *Le déclin de l'empire américain* and *Jésus de Montréal*. In the field of short films, Frédéric Back is especially loved. He produced animation shorts for Radio-Canada, two of which won Oscars: *Crac!* (1981) an original and endearing illustration of the Quebec culture and *L'homme qui plantait des arbres* (1988), taken from a Jean Giono novella.

Conclusion

All in all, the 1960s and the *Révoluton tranquille* brought momentous changes in the literary and artistic world of Quebec, a world trying to detach itself from its old constraints: the clergy, the past, and the conservative ideologies that had been more or less sustaining it until then. Instead of considering itself as a part of French literature, the Quebec literary world was assuming its specificity by creating a national literature with its own traditions and its own revolutionary growth. After the slow improvements observed in the 1940s, the institutional modernization launched by the province during the Quiet Revolution increased not only the consumption of goods by the public and the creation of new facilities, but also the upgrading of artists' and writers' living conditions and the betterment and diversification of all types of artist productions. Infrastructures were set in place to reform the area and catch up with the modern times. Now, more books, music, and artworks are being produced and sold than ever before, both nationally and internationally.

Nonetheless, despite the major changes taking place on the *Québécois* soil, its historical past was never obliterated from literature; it was transcended, worked around, and sometimes used to reinforce the francophone community's origins, but history was never far from the collective memory. "*Je me souviens*," Quebec's motto, confirms it. In the 1970s, a spirit of independence and of being a distinct nation anchored itself among politicians and intellectuals who promoted laws toward the conservation of the French language as the primary language of the province. The Parti Québécois, a new political party, was founded in 1968 by René Lévesque, a man who went on to become Prime Minister of Quebec and who firmly believed in the notions of sovereignty and of separatism. Two referendums in 1980 and 1995 were initiated. Both failed to pass by a very small margin. Thus, the question still remains as to whether Quebec is to become a nation of its own, apart from the rest of Canada, or whether it will maintain its present provincial status. Despite these lingering questions, one thing is certain: Quebec wishes to retain its distinction and its French language and appears willing, as in the past, to fight for them.

REFERENCES

Bersianik, Louky. *L'Euguélionne*. Montréal: Stanké, 1985.

Canada-Québec-Synthèse historique. Montréal: Éds. du Renouveau Pédagogique Inc., 1978.

Giguère, Roland. *Rose and Thorn, Selected Poems of Roland Giguère*. Trans. Donald Winkler. Toronto: Exile Editions, 1988.

Godbout, Jacques. *Hail Galarneau!* Trans. Alan Brown. Don Mills, Ontario: Longman Canada Limited, 1970.

Hémon, Louis. *Maria Chapdelaine*. Trans. W. H. Blake. Illus. Thoreau MacDonald. Toronto: The Macmillan Company, 1948.

Histoire du Québec contemporain. De la Confédération à la crise. (1867-1929). Montréal: Boréal Express, 1979.

Histoire du Québec contemporain. Le Québec depuis 1930. Montréal: Boréal Express, 1986.

Jack, Belinda. *Francophone Literatures: An Introductory Survey*. Oxford: Oxford UP, 1996.

Mailhot, Laurent, *La Littérature québécoise*, coll. *Que sais-je ?*. Paris: PUF, 1975.

Mailhot, Laurent, and Pierre Nepveu. *La Poésie québécoise. Anthologie*. Montréal: TYPO, 1990.

Joubert, J.-L., et al. *Les Littératures francophones depuis 1945*. Paris: Bordas, 1986.

Nelligan, Émile. *Selected Poems*. Trans. P. F. Widdows. Toronto: The Ryerson P, 1960.

Roy, Gabrielle. *The Tin Flute*. Trans. Hannah Josephson. Toronto: McClelland & Stewart, Ltd., 1947.

Tétu de Labsade, Françoise. *Le Québec: un pays, une culture*. Montréal: Boréal, 1990.

Tremblay, Michel. *Les Belles-Soeurs*. Trans. John Van Burek and Bill Glasco. Vancouver: Talonbooks, 1974.

Marie-Paule Méda

DISCUSSION QUESTIONS

1. What aspects of this article on Quebec's culture and civilization surprised or confounded you the most? Why?

2. Isolate and discuss some factors that kept Quebec from evolving at the rate of other industrialized countries.

3. Is Quebec right in its fight for sovereignty? Does a language purport that much importance so as to initiate a separation?

4. As an anglophone, how does your past compare to that of francophones in Quebec?

5. In the same situation, would you be willing to fight for the right to keep your language from being invaded by another?

6. How would you resolve Quebec's problem?

❖❖ CHAPTER NINE
❖ The Francophone Presence
in the Northeastern United States

Janet L. Shideler

At the turn of the last century, many French-Canadian and Franco-American journalists, novelists, and poets made the observation that the separation of compatriots on both sides of the Canada-United States border was of a momentary nature. They clung to the conviction that the distance between French Canadians and their diaspora in the Northeastern United States was a temporary phenomenon. In the view of Camille Lessard-Bissonnette and Edmond de Nevers, for example, time would correct the tragedy of their separation, and the two peoples would soon be one again. Rather than considering whether these writers were making an informed observation or were offering an optimistic prediction, a most compelling story, that of the departure of hundreds of thousands who left their *patrie*, Quebec, and of their very different fates, begs to be told.

It is in this first task, that of examining precisely what it was that urged a massive exodus of French Canadians for the United States, that one discovers that Franco-Americans were not unlike "pioneers" throughout North America. Movement meant possible opportunities to be found. As historian Marcus Hansen explains in speaking of immigration as a very generalized activity:

> The crossing and recrossing of the boundary were not part of a haphazard, aimless wandering. They represented a search for the opportunities offered by land, factories and cities . . . The farmer emigrating from east to west, the artisan in search of a factory job, the young man looking for a position in a bank or office, viewed the continent as a whole. They sought neither the United States nor Canada, but America and opportunity.[1]

Most especially for those of us for whom the northernmost stretches of the Northeastern United States are home, Hansen's remarks ring true. So accustomed are we to sharing our existence with Canadians that, even in the dead of winter, the St. Lawrence River, the waterway separating us from our northern neighbor, seems a most "fluid" boundary in every sense of the word. For those of us separated by dry land whose topography and climate scarcely suggest that a change of venue is taking place, an inspection at Customs and Immigration, in either direction, is a formality. However they identify themselves, as Canadian or American, there is a sense for many who cross the border that their past, if not their present also, must have been intrinsically linked to that of inhabitants of the neighboring nation. For Franco-Americans, the largest ethnic group in many counties and communities throughout the Northeastern United States, this is indeed the case.

What, then, occurred in the past? Why did French Canadians arrive at the conclusion that opportunity would be best sought elsewhere? Theirs is a story of fear of reprisals arising from the Rebellion of 1837–38. In fleeing to northern New York and northern Vermont especially, French-Canadian *patriotes* were able to escape an unsympathetic government.[2] Their story is also one of despair in response to increasing hopelessness in French Canada and one of hope in response to a need for manpower in the United States.

In short, three concrete factors on the rise in Quebec in the mid-1800s would encourage the departure of French Canadians for the United States: unemployment, seasonal employment, and the minimal yields of agriculture. Again in northern New York and northern Vermont, in particular, many French Canadian farmers would continue their lives as farmers but would do so in the hope of better returns from other land. For still others, growing up in a province whose population had been taught that agriculture was not only the most viable but also the most blessed of vocations, leaving that way of life behind had become an absolute, unavoidable necessity. Farm owners were buried in debt. They faced mortgages upon their land, the deterioration of soil often tilled by the same family for generation after generation, the impossibility of acquiring new lands whose purchase prices were beyond their grasp, and a government that did little to address problems of outmoded agricultural techniques or poor access to markets. All of these factors added up, not only to an eagerness to earn an assured, year-round income elsewhere, but also, in more instances than we can estimate, to a deliberate choice to abandon a way of life that many had come to despise.

Meanwhile, the manufacturing towns and cities of the New England states, in particular, urgently required not only skilled labor but also, and more significantly, unskilled labor. In this regard, the emigration of *Québécois* for the United States constituted not only a wave of immigration like any other global one, but also a people's determination to write its own destiny. One must never ignore the singular significance of this event in Quebec history, for it reveals a bold debunking of the myth of the gloriously contented and divinely blessed *habitant*.[3]

As one speaks of the employment opportunities south of the border, that is not to suggest that a manufacturing sector was not present in the Province of Quebec. Indeed, as demographer Yolande Lavoie points out in her noteworthy study of emigration of French Canadians to the United States, statistics suggest that because the city of Montreal was the departure point for many emigrants, there might have been fewer emigrants from among the agrarian class than one had presumed. However, as she explains and as researchers now know, many of these working-class, urban emigrants had first gone to the city to try their hand at manufacturing there before moving on to the more abundant opportunities to the South.[4]

It also bears repeating that not only farmers left for the United States. Where there was business, there were growing communities. Moreover, where there were growing communities; there was a need for a new infrastructure and hence the possibility of building one's work around the provision of services in this new infrastructure. It follows, then, that not all French-Canadian immigrants were poor, mortgage-burdened farmers whose only "possession" was an extraordinary willingness to work hard for minimal wages. The wave of migration and the subsequent growth of New England towns and cities also carried with it a French-Canadian bourgeoisie: journalists, doctors, shopkeepers, and bankers. This was a class of individuals ready to share growing prosperity with Yankees, but before they would do that, they already felt a certain degree of optimism concerning their prospects for success. They had an eager clientele ready to conduct business in their *langue maternelle*, their "mother tongue": French.

It should be noted that this was not a particularly wealthy middle class. For many, their debts in Canada were almost as crushing as those of their agricultural counterparts destined for the mills and factories. But if they shared an uncertain past, they also shared with their compatriots a desire to leave that past behind and forge what might be a very different future.

It is no surprise, then, that with broad representation from various social classes, it took little time for French-Canadian communities to appear in cities and towns throughout the Northeastern United States. Virtually every urban region that boasted a textile mill, a shoe manufacturing plant or other industries in need of "cheap labor" also became home to a *Petit Canada*. It is still possible for visitors traveling to cities such as Manchester, New Hampshire; Lowell, Massachusetts; Holyoke, Massachusetts; Lewiston, Maine; Woonsocket, Rhode Island; and others, to find the Little Canadas of these cities. Moreover, one still frequently meets *Francos* throughout those cities for whom French is, if not their primary language, certainly a language that is integral to their daily life.[5]

It is not entirely surprising either that *le fait français*, the "French fact", should make itself felt in the Northeastern United States. Many, though not all, French Canadians (or *Franco-Americans* as they would be called shortly after 1900) were determined to transplant social institutions that clearly resembled the *patrie* or the homeland that they left behind. Churches in which the Roman Catholicism of their forefathers could be freely practiced and confessions heard in the language of their own people abounded, not merely in one or two towns, but in virtually every urban center where French Canadians laid down roots. In this regard, immigrants from French Canada scarcely differed from those whose places of origin were much more distant. Separate churches for German, French, Polish, Lithuanian, and other ethnic immigrant groups were reminders of growing ethnic diversity in the United States.

However, as much as *langue* and *foi*, language and faith, seem to have been inextricably linked at this time in French-Canadian and *Franco-American* history, the use of the mother tongue was not merely restricted to the profession of one's faith. Mutual aid societies, newspapers, and schools in which daily affairs were conducted in French were the hallmark of what had been, to that point, largely Yankee towns and cities. From these same towns and cities emerged more than 250 French-language newspapers, although some would eventually evolve into bilingual or predominantly English publications still written for a *Franco* readership and aimed at assuring the survival of *Franco* culture in the United States.[6]

There is no question that the proximity of the homeland gave French Canadians a very distinct advantage over other ethnic groups who had arrived. Over one-tenth of Quebec's population—conservative estimates suggest one-and-a-half million—departed for the United States between 1830 and 1930, making their mere numbers a formidable presence.[7] Yet, in the eyes of those to whose long-established communities they came, French Canadians appeared to be determined not to adopt and to adapt, but rather to establish their own institutions, values, and language.

It is perhaps small wonder, then, that resentment toward French-Canadian immigrants should manifest itself both privately and publicly. French-Canadian immigrants were almost exclusively Roman Catholic, making them papists. Moreover, theirs was a particularly conservative brand of Catholicism wherein the Church dominated much of the group's way of thinking and behaving. Diligence in work and submission to one's employer were the order of the day, in sharp contrast to rising labor activism. French Canadians were frequently accused of undercutting the efforts of other workers (including other French Canadians) to improve salaries and working conditions by their willingness to accept inconceivably low wages for their labor. Criticism was also leveled against them for their alleged tendency to falsify records concerning the age of children so that even the youngest family members might seek employment. In an industry where the labor of children and women was in special demand because of the delicacy of their hands and their subsequent handiwork (namely in the textile industry) many Yankee and immigrant families sent their children to the mill instead of sending them to school.

Nevertheless, French Canadians were often singled out as the greatest violator of child labor laws. The implication was not only that this immigrant group was the most eager to defy the laws of its country of adoption, but also that its members were clearly the most exploitative and the most guilty of neglecting the welfare of children. The Connecticut Bureau of Labor Statistics offered this scathing observation in its annual report for the year 1885:

> Another element, which affects child labor, is that of race. The native American (i.e., born and raised in the United States) almost always wants to educate his children. The Irishman feels this want even more strongly, and will make great sacrifices for the sake of his family. On the other hand, the French Canadian, in a great many instances, regards his children as a means of adding to the earning capacity of his family, and, in making arrangements for work, he urges, and even insists upon the employment of the family as a whole, down to the very youngest children who can be of any possible service.[8]

In defense of the French-Canadians, some historians suggest that the high instance of child labor among Franco-American families was the result of the "transplanted" belief that mill labor—much like field labor on the farm in Quebec—was of far more benefit to their children's future than was a formal education, since labor ensured eventual self-sufficiency. In addition, in the French-Canadian social structure, the father, as *chef* or head of the household, was said to hold a divinely granted right and responsibility to determine what was best for the welfare of the entire family unit. The employment of even the youngest family members was not viewed as exploitation or as defiance of new laws, but rather as the fulfillment of duty as well as the recognition of tradition.

Finally, there is much evidence to suggest that some of the accusations launched against Franco-Americans on this issue were the result of bias against this ethnic community. The Report of the Immigration Commission, released in 1905, noted that, among cotton millworkers that year, Irish children contributed 45% to the overall income in families who were surveyed, whereas the contribution of French-Canadian children to their families accounted for only one-third of the overall income.[9]

This view of Franco-Americans and of the value they chose to place on education is one that could be and, indeed, still is being disputed. What is irrefutable, however, is the astounding number of French Canadians (men, women, boys and girls) who were in the workplace throughout the New England states. Theirs was an extraordinarily conspicuous presence:

> The French Canadians made themselves felt in this industry [cotton textile] in the 1870s, when there were over 7,000 Canadian-born engaged in it in New England. Within thirty years, this number soared to nearly 60,000. French-Canadian operatives in cotton rose from 20% to nearly 37% of the total number in Massachusetts between 1890 and 1900, and in Maine and New Hampshire they exceeded 60%. In 1888 over 3,000 French-Canadian women were employed in the cotton mills of Lewiston, Biddeford, Saco, and Waterville [Maine], out of a total of approximately five and a half thousand female employees.[10]

It would be impossible to overstate the significance of this development in the social history of French Canada. The proletarization of women would certainly not remain unheard of in the Province of Quebec, particularly in the city of Montreal where the manufacturing industry, as already noted, would lure many rural families away from agriculture as a source of income and introduce virtually all family members to the phenomenon of salaried labor. The *Québécoise*'s or French Canadian woman's counterpart in the United States, however, would do so earlier and with considerably more vigor. Moreover, the *Franco-Américaine* stepped into the workplace in the milltowns of New England following the departure of Yankee "millgirls." There was, therefore, a precedent for this new group of women and young girls in industry, even though, as one must acknowledge, immigrant women did not enjoy the widespread approval of their participation in labor that their English-speaking, native-born sisters had.

Yet another criticism was leveled against French-Canadian immigrants, namely that their efforts to improve their economic lot were conducted at the exclusion of making financial contributions to their adopted homeland, the United States. Some believed that these were foreigners whose attachment still lay elsewhere and who, because of the subsequent detachment from the nation that had generously received them, were bent on taking from the United States without giving anything back in return. In an epithet created specifically for French Canadians by the Massachusetts Office of Labor Statistics but quickly adopted by the larger public, the sting of resentment against them and against another large and equally hardworking group of immigrants can still be felt. They were called "*les Chinois de l'Est*" or "the Chinese of the East." Just as Chinese workers in the western United States were charged with working for their own benefit and sending any profits back to their loved ones in China in order that their lot might also be improved, so too, were French Canadians sharply criticized for these actions, which were viewed as a refusal to declare a single loyalty. "Canucks," as they were also termed, were industrial invaders, determined to remain in the United States just long enough to make a profit for themselves and their compatriots in Quebec before returning to their native land.

To add fuel to the defensively nationalistic fire, the Little Canadas of New England milltowns were regularly cited as being the filthiest of various cities' neighborhoods. They were attacked for overcrowded and unsafe conditions; it was asserted, although most often without statistics to support the accusation, that the Little Canadas constituted the most densely populated tenement districts in all of the United States. Ironically, French Canadians, upon their arrival in New England towns and cities, did not build their own dwellings, but rather they lived in the housing projects constructed specifically by mill owners for their laborers. Furthermore, there is no question that sanitation was precarious at best in these sections of the city, but there is little, if any, evidence to suggest that French-Canadian immigrants could be singled out for creating and living in squalor. New England's *Petits Canadas* were home to some of the region's most exquisite Roman Catholic churches, built as a result of tremendous financial sacrifice on the part of French-Canadian immigrants. The beauty of these edifices in the midst of alleged indifference to living conditions is ironic. The irony continues because, although these churches were clearly a testimony to the willingness and, indeed, the fervent desire of a people to remain and to put down roots in this adopted homeland, the very presence of these temples of the Roman Catholic faith was worrisome to many Yankees who shared cities and towns with these relative newcomers. The *Commercial Advertiser of New York* warned, in 1890, that descendants of the Pilgrims, the "true" founders of New England, were steadily being outnumbered by the descendants of a people who had fallen to the British on the Plains of Abraham. The "English race," the publication warned, was being replaced by the "French race."[11]

To the reader of that day, the term "race" carried with it some very specific connotations. Belonging to a "race" implied that a people had innate characteristics, such as the religion they practiced, the language they spoke, how prolific members were, and the ambitions they pursued. In short, members of various races were born with a predisposition to certain beliefs, traditions, and practices. Those born into the French-Canadian race were seen to be, by nature, devout followers of the Pope, given to high birth rates that numerically would threaten any other "race," ferociously determined to preserve and spread the French language, which was, after all, intrinsically linked to faith, and committed to forming a community unto themselves which might thereby resist assimilation.

One can dispute whether or not French Canadians ever truly heeded the lesson of *messianisme* or evangelization that had been preached to them by their religious leadership in Quebec, which urged them to spread their language and faith throughout North America. What is irrefutable, however, is that many others looking in at this community were clearly convinced that this was a people with a mission and that their mission was a most nefarious one.

French-Canadians (or Franco-Americans as they would increasingly call themselves shortly after 1900) were not unaware of the fears and even the hostility that their presence provoked in the larger community surrounding them. In fact, they even came under fire from within the ranks of the Roman Catholic Church in New England, largely led by Irish bishops, who singled them out as clinging too devotedly to the French language. The interconnectedness of French-language churches and schools was seen as a source of divisiveness among followers of one faith but also, in more concrete terms, as a threat to resources required to advance that faith. In the case of the Sentinelle affair in Woonsocket, Rhode Island, in the 1920s, for example, French-Canadian believers were forced to choose between support of the Roman Catholic education as a whole, to be conducted in English, or Roman Catholic education to be carried out in French. For many, their support of the latter resulted in being branded as traitors or, at the very least, as selfish individuals unwilling to sacrifice their own interests in the name of the advancement of the Church. Such disobedience was surely not in keeping with the tenets of the faith. In their defense, many Franco-Americans viewed the painful choice between language and faith as being a wholly unnecessary one, forced upon them by assimilationists who were not Protestants, but Irish Roman Catholics.

There would be yet another choice that would be urged upon French Canadians who had immigrated to the United States: naturalization versus repatriation. As for the latter, there was an official effort, made by the Quebec government to lure expatriates back to the *mère-patrie*, which included the possibility of land grants. It is estimated that more than 100,000 French Canadians and descendants of emigrants did, in fact, return to Quebec. Still others accepted land grant incentives in the Canadian West, and many found their way to the neighboring province of Ontario. Some would return to the United States once again following that nation's recovery from the Depression. That economic event was to have the single most significant influence on immigration, emigration, and repatriation, outweighing the rhetoric of politicians espousing repatriation. The "Crash" of 1929 would effectively close places of entry, and for perhaps the first time in their history as a workforce, French Canadians would not be uniquely desirable as the docile, capable workforce they had appeared to be in the earlier days when recruiting agents actually sought them out in Quebec. This was before Franco-Americans, along with other workers, would become involved in labor activism. More importantly, though, the Depression meant that there was, after all, no new job creation for would-be workers, however willing they might be to accept minimal wages in grueling conditions.

As in its earliest days, the flux and reflux over the Canada-United States border and the French Canadian presence in the United States had more to do in most instances with the search for economic opportunity and survival than it ever did with patriotism. On the other hand, patriotism had a major role to play in naturalization. Beginning in the 1880s and 1890s in particular, the French-Canadian press in the United States—who actually created the term Franco-American in an effort to more aptly describe the new standing of French Canadians in the United States—discussed the issue at length in its columns. In general, journalists were in support of this change of status in nationality. Fraternal and mutual aid societies hosted conferences where naturalization was frequently the topic, and those who attended were encouraged to join the growing ranks of French Canadians who were assuming United States citizenship. Many responded affirmatively to the call to become "American." For many French-Canadian immigrants, their adopted land had evolved into their home of choice. Time and integration into a new way of living would, in a sense, triumph over lingering nostalgia.

Moreover, there were clearly benefits to be derived from declaring one's allegiance to this adopted country. Women who opted to become naturalized citizens of the United States were granted the right to vote in 1920, a full twenty years before their counterparts would be given this same right in provincial elections in Quebec. One must not surmise from this that the women's suffrage movement was without opposition in the United States for, indeed, it encountered much. However, women's right to vote was unquestionably viewed with more favor in the United States than it was in French Canada at the time, and there is little doubt that French-Canadian immigrant women were aware of this, given the proximity of their homeland and ongoing news coverage of events there via the Franco-American press.

In any case, Franco-Americans in general wasted little time before becoming involved in the politics of regions where their ethnic group had long been either a majority or a considerable presence. Widespread involvement of *Francos* brought them into positions of considerable influence, including being elected as mayors, senators, and representatives.

For the children and grandchildren of French-Canadian immigrants, there was little question as to where they "belonged," even though institutions such as schools, churches, and associations would remind them of their roots. Franco-American parochial schools throughout the Northeast offered instruction in both French and English, with the day generally divided in half concerning the language of instruction, while Canadian history and geography also remained part of the standard curriculum at most of these schools until the 1940s and sometimes until the 1950s.

That period (the 1940s) would mark a turning point in the identity and attachments of Franco-Americans. Events such as World War I, but especially World War II, would be instrumental in urging immigrants, not just French Canadians, to declare their loyalties. Ultimately, most would opt for a future firmly established in the United States. In the words of singer-songwriter, Josée Vachon, singing in 1984, "*Je ne suis plus Canayenne, mais Franco-Américaine*" ("I am no longer Canadian, but Franco-American").[12]

It is important to note, however, that if naturalization meant "Americanization" of French Canadians and their descendants in the United States, it does not necessarily follow that total assimilation has been the outcome of this change in status. While it is true that the use of French language, once the tie that bound most *Francos* together, is clearly on the decline, many Franco-Americans derive hope from a continued and, more significantly, a renewed interest in *Franco-américanie*. Museums and resource centers aimed at preserving and promoting the culture of Franco-Americans not only exist, but are once again increasing in number, thanks to the determination of an ethnic group whose members once faced derision for displaying the differences that they now celebrate.

The literature of this sizeable French-Canadian "diaspora" is the subject of research that is growing at a rapid pace. More traditional Franco-American writers and those who were *Franco* writers in New England for a time have become topics of renewed studies. They include Louis Dantin, Honoré Beaugrand, Rosaire Dion-Lévesque, Alberte Gastonguay, Camille Lessard-Bissonnette, Anna-Marie Duval-Thibault and Jacques Ducharme, to name just a few. In addition, students of ethnic studies are casting new light on readings of the works of *Francos* like Jack Kerouac and Grace Metalious. As for evidence of literature that still emerges from this community, E. Annie Proulx and Clark Blaise are perhaps two of the best known Franco-American authors of our time, but they certainly are not the only ones. In addition, folklorists, musicians, poets, and playwrights abound and tell (sadly with less and less frequency in French) the proud tale of a people who, despite criticism from the homeland and their adopted country, went on to make considerable contributions to their new communities and to write their own story. Franco-American associations and organizations live on, and their membership is not, as some would suggest, derived solely from an "older generation" of *Francos*.

Relevant to the issue of language maintenance, it is noteworthy that French immersion opportunities are surfacing in some regions of the Northeast as well as within what were once French-speaking communities in Louisiana. At the same time, Franco-Americans are grappling with what will be perhaps the most difficult and challenging question posed to them in their long and proud history: is it necessary that a language remain intact in order for a people to assert that its culture is still alive and vibrant? Whatever the answer, one can be certain that just as when they chose to emigrate, to earn wages in an unfamiliar workplace using an even more unfamiliar language, to build institutions that would preserve their way of life in the face of enormous criticism, to integrate themselves into new communities, and to take on a new national identity, Franco-Americans are resolved to answer this question on their own terms.

NOTES

1. Marcus Lee Hansen, *The Immigrant in American History* (New York: Harper & Row, 1940), 190.

2. The choice of the term is a curious one: the *patriotes* were rebels whose opposition to an allegedly "irresponsible" government, imposed by Great Britain, ironically earned them the English title of patriots rather than traitors. In addition to their forced exodus to the United States, these rebels were also exiled to Australia and a dozen were hanged for treason.

3. The term *habitant* has changed meanings through the years. From a term aimed simply at naming someone who occupied the land but who enjoyed a status that was slightly more elevated than that of a peasant, the *habitant* came to be regarded as the incarnation of the *Québécois'* love of the land, of family, of the French language, and of the Roman Catholic faith.

4. Yolande Lavoie, *L'émigration des Québécois aux Etats-Unis de 1840 à 1930* (Québec: Editeur officiel du Québec, 1981), 17.

5. The term *Franco-Américain* or *Franco* is believed to have originated in the newspaper, *L'Opinion Publique*, at the turn of the century in an effort to find an expression that depicted both the ethnic and linguistic origins of a people whose identification was increasingly with the United States.

6. Normand Lafleur, *Les "Chinois de l'est"* (Montréal: Leméac, 1981), 75.

7. Jacques Rouillard, *Ah les Etats!* (Montréal: Boréal Express, 1985), 11.

8. The 1885 Report of the Connecticut Bureau of Labor Statistics, quoted by Iris Saunders Podea, "Quebec to 'Little Canada': The Coming of the French Canadians to New England in the Nineteenth Century," *New England Quarterly* (September 1950): 374–75.

9. Saunders Podea, 374–75.

10. Saunders Podea, 369–70.

11. *The Commercial Advertiser of New York* (October 1890), quoted by Edouard Hamon, S.J., *Les Canadiens-français de la Nouvelle-Angleterre* (Quebec: N.-S. Hardy, 1891), 151.

12. Josée Vachon, "Entre moi," 1984.

DISCUSSION QUESTIONS

1. Efforts to control or regularize immigration into the United States are not a recent phenomenon. What are some of the questions and controversies currently surrounding immigration policies? Do you see possible parallels with policies in place earlier in this century?

2. How do you feel that immigration to the United States, particularly from regions shaped by traditionalism, conservatism, and poverty might have influenced the lives and roles of various family members as well as the structure of the family itself?

3. As mentioned in this article, a comparison was drawn between Chinese immigrants on the West Coast and French-Canadian immigrants in the northeastern United States. Examine this comparison in greater depth. Was this an accurate comparison?

4. Study the histories of Franco-Americans of the Northeast and Cajuns in Louisiana in greater depth. What similarities/differences can you uncover in their experiences as francophones forging new lives in the United States?

5. Examine the linguistic phenomenon of how family names of immigrants are transformed by translation, phonetics, etc. Why does this change in identity occur, and what are its implications for an immigrant?

❖ CONTRIBUTORS

Debra L. Anderson currently teaches French and francophone literature at East Carolina University. She is the author of *Decolonizing the Text: Glissantian Readings in Caribbean and African-American Literatures* (Peter Lang, 1995). Her research interests include comparative studies of French Caribbean, African-American, and Southern writers.

Michelle Beauclair received her B.S.L.A. in French from Georgetown University in Washington, DC, and her M.A. and Ph.D. in French literature from the University of Wisconsin-Madison. She teaches French and francophone culture courses at Edmonds Community College in Lynnwood, WA, and advanced francophone literature courses at Seattle Pacific University. She has also taught a francophone course in Paris for the Washington Consortium of Community Colleges. She is the author of *Albert Camus, Marguerite Duras, and the Legacy of Mourning* (Peter Lang, 1998).

Sylvie Charron received her doctoral degree in French literature from the University of Wisconsin and is an associate professor of French at the University of Maine at Farmington. She has published numerous essays on the works of George Sand and has served as guest editor for the journal *George Sand Studies*. Most of her research centers on issues of class and gender in the nineteenth century. She and Sue Huseman both participated in the group translation of George Sand's *Story of My Life: The Autobiography of George Sand*. They collaborated on a translation of George Sand's *La Marquise* and *Pauline* and on a translation of Tahar Ben Jelloun's *Les Raisins de la galère*.

Beverley G. David, a native of Guyana, received her M.A. in French from the University of British Columbia in Vancouver, Canada. She has studied in Guyana, France, and Canada. Her research interests include the francophone cultures of Africa, the West Indies, and French Guiana. She currently serves as a senior instructor of French at the University of Wisconsin-Stevens Point where she has received the University Excellence in Teaching Award. She also holds a diploma in French translation and is a freelance translator of technical documents.

Sue Huseman received a doctoral degree in comparative literature from the University of Illinois and is currently serving as Vice Chancellor for Academic Affairs for the University of Maine System. She has served as President for the University of Maine at Farmington and Monmouth College in Illinois. She has taught language and literature, interpreted and translated literary texts, and explored issues of gender and cultural differences within the academy and society at large. In collaboration with Sylvie Charron, she translated George Sand's *La Marquise* and *Pauline* and Tahar Ben Jelloun's *Les Raisins de la galère* and participated in the group translation of George Sand's *Story of My Life: The Autobiography of George Sand*.

Paschal B. Kyiiripuo Kyoore acquired his B.A. degree in French and Spanish at the University of Ghana-Legon, and his M.A. and Diplôme d'Etudes Approfondies in French and comparative literature at the Centre d'Etudes Littéraires Maghrébines, Africaines et Antillaises (C.E.L.M.A.) of the Université de Bordeaux III (France). His Ph.D. in Romance Languages and Literatures is from the Ohio State University. He is an associate professor of French at Gustavus Adolphus College in Saint Peter, Minnesota. He specializes in francophone African and Caribbean literatures and cultures, as well as French literature of the nineteenth and twentieth centuries. Dr. Kyoore is the author of *The African and Caribbean Historical Novel in French: A Quest for Identity* (Peter Lang, 1996).

Marie-Paule Méda received her B.A. in French and education and her M.A. in French literature from the University of Washington, Seattle, and her Ph.D. in francophone literature from the University of British Columbia, Vancouver. She has taught French and francophone literature courses at Western Washington University, Everett Community College, and at the Alliance Française of Seattle. She has delivered numerous presentations and published articles on French Canadian culture and literature.

Marcia G. Parker earned her B.A. in French from Lawrence University, Appleton, WI, and her M.A. and Ph.D. in French from the University of Wisconsin-Madison, specializing in nineteenth- and twentieth-century francophone theater. She holds the rank of associate professor of French at the University of Wisconsin-Stevens Point where she was the recipient of the University Excellence in Teaching Award. In addition to numerous other awards for distinguished teaching, she has published and presented many articles on teaching and French theater, and recently co-authored *Générations*, a French writing text.

Alain Péricard obtained his Ph.D. from McGill University in Montreal where he is currently an adjunct professor in the Graduate Program in Communications. He has worked in journalism and in development in Africa for fifteen years. Currently he is doing research on intercultural and organizational communication in francophone West Africa. He has published numerous articles on development, the environment, and the mass media in Africa.

Timothy Scheie received his B.A. from St. Olaf College, and his M.A. and Ph.D. in French from the University of Wisconsin-Madison. He is an associate professor of French at the Eastman School of Music, Rochester, NY. His research and teaching interests include French theater and literature, performance theory, and language instruction. He has published numerous articles on the theater and is the recipient of several prestigious fellowships including the Bridging Fellowship and the Markham Fellowship.

Susan Stringer, a native of England, has undergraduate degrees from Australia and France in French, German, history, and linguistics, an M.A. in French from the University of London, and a Ph.D. in French and German from the University of Colorado. She has also completed graduate courses in Latin American literature in Spanish. Her specialization is women's writing from Senegal, and she is the author of *The Senegalese Novel by Women* (Peter Lang, 1996). She currently teaches at the Universidad de Los Lagos in Osorno, Chile.

Janet L. Shideler resides in the northeastern United States and is the author of *Camille Lessard-Bissonnette: The Quiet Evolution of French-Canadian Immigrants in New England* (Peter Lang, 1998).

FRANCOPHONE CULTURES & LITERATURES

General Editors: Michael G. Paulson & Tamara Alvarez-Detrell

The Francophone Cultures and Literatures series encompasses studies about the literature, culture, and civilization of the Francophone areas of Africa, Asia, Europe, the Americas, the French-speaking islands in the Caribbean, as well as French Canada. Cross-cultural studies between and among these geographic areas are encouraged. The book-length manuscripts may be written in either English or French.

For further information about the Francophone Cultures and Literatures series and for the submission of manuscripts, contact:

Michael G. Paulson
Tamara Alvarez-Detrell
c/o Dr. Heidi Burns
Peter Lang Publishing, Inc.
P.O. Box 1246
Bel Air, MD 21014-1246

To order other books in this series, please contact our Customer Service Department:

(800) 770-LANG (within the U.S.)
(212) 647-7706 (outside the U.S.)
(212) 647-7707 FAX

or browse online by series at:

WWW.PETERLANG.COM